MAVERICK FEMINIST

MAVERICK FEMINIST

To Be Female and Black in a Country Founded
upon Violence and Respectability

Kemeshia Randle Swanson

University Press of Mississippi / Jackson

The University Press of Mississippi is the scholarly publishing agency of the Mississippi Institutions of Higher Learning: Alcorn State University, Delta State University, Jackson State University, Mississippi State University, Mississippi University for Women, Mississippi Valley State University, University of Mississippi, and University of Southern Mississippi.

www.upress.state.ms.us

The University Press of Mississippi is a member
of the Association of University Presses.

∞

Library of Congress Cataloging-in-Publication Data

Names: Swanson, Kemeshia Randle, author.
Title: Maverick feminist : to be female and Black in a country founded upon violence and respectability / Kemeshia Randle Swanson.
Description: Jackson : University Press of Mississippi, 2024. | Includes bibliographical references and index.
Identifiers: LCCN 2023042347 (print) | LCCN 2023042348 (ebook) | ISBN 9781496850645 (hardback) | ISBN 9781496850652 (trade paperback) | ISBN 9781496850669 (epub) | ISBN 9781496850676 (epub) | ISBN 9781496850683 (pdf) | ISBN 9781496850690 (pdf)
Subjects: LCSH: Women, Black—Social conditions. | African American women—Social conditions. | Women, Black—Sexual behavior. | African American women—Sexual behavior. | African American feminists. | Feminism. | Feminism and racism.
Classification: LCC HQ1163 .S93 2024 (print) | LCC HQ1163 (ebook) | DDC 305.48/896073—dc23/eng/20231030
LC record available at https://lccn.loc.gov/2023042347
LC ebook record available at https://lccn.loc.gov/2023042348

British Library Cataloging-in-Publication Data available

This book is dedicated to every girl or woman who has ever been told what they shouldn't say or do for fear of what someone else might say or do. I hear you. I see you. I love you. I support you.

CONTENTS

MAVERICK FEMINIST

RECLAIMING MY EVERYTHING

Black Feminisms, Popular Culture, and Pleasure

Funk, then, is not only as Toni Morrison has stated, the opposite of black bourgeois repression of pleasure and spontaneity,
but also an effective technology that can sustain reciprocal
interactions that would improve the lives of women and, in the
end, the men and children in their lives.
—L. H. STALLINGS, *FUNK THE EROTIC: TRANSAESTHETICS AND
BLACK SEXUAL CULTURES* (2015)

I became a feminist during the spring of 2010 while sitting in Brittney
Cooper's Black Feminist Thought class at the predominately white
University of Alabama. Before this particular course, I had no personal
relationships with people who openly identified as Black feminists—at
least none that I was aware of. Needless to say, radical feminists were
not showing up at my doorstep or on the street corners of my Mississippi Delta town preaching the word of "Thus Saith the Lorde."[1]
And, if I am being honest, the readings assigned by Cooper early in
the semester, even Audre Lorde's, did not immediately convince me
that I should be gung ho about joining the bandwagon. Of course,
now, I honor and respect Mother Audre, Beverly Guy-Sheftall, and all
of the women accounted for in her work *Words of Fire: An Anthology of African-American Feminist Thought* (1995). However, I am not
ashamed to admit that I was less enthralled during the first half of
the course and was still quite hesitant to adopt the feminist label. It
was not until I was introduced to Joan Morgan's memoir-manifesto
that I was redeemed.

The unflinchingly provocative account of Morgan's journey to feminism, as detailed in *When Chickenheads Come Home to Roost* (1999), was, for me, as it was for so many other young women, an entrée into the world of Black feminisms. After completing only a few pages of the text, I opened myself up to be a willing vessel, and the Black feminist goddesses came down from heaven and welcomed me into the fold. I was reborn as a woman with heightened confidence and minimal fears. Morgan's work, with its Hip Hop–esque prose, while not more valuable than Anna Julia Cooper's, Mary Church Terrell's, or Ida B. Wells-Barnett's, simply spoke more effervescently to my *boughetto* upbringing.[2] It was like a breath of fresh air, as it acknowledged that around the way girls had power and influence too; Morgan was a feminist who admitted that there were some things about patriarchy that she appreciated, a feminist who insisted that being a feminist and being strong should not be a death sentence. Even more, her work helped me to gain an appreciation for its precursors and for those that would follow.

Unaware of the amount of work required to make this journey and lifestyle fruitful for myself and others, I came out kicking and screaming, ready to take on the world in contemporary feminist armor: "Big brown lips in the most decadent of shades, [a] phat ass [piled into a] micromini, [and] freshly manicured toes [in] four-inch fuck-me sandals" (Joan Morgan 57). I felt like a superhero with life-changing powers, an impactful voice, and a serious job to do, but I quickly realized that I had to be my own first subject, so after my *awakening*, I began, more thoroughly, to evaluate my past as well as my present and imagine a future that was more fruitful and free.

During my self-explorations, I concluded that as an ambitious young girl growing up in Holmes County, Mississippi—interestingly, the poorest county in the poorest state in the country—I was not simply raised in a strict household; I was a product of the school of respectability. While freedom was always appealing, funk, fuck, and feminism did not sit well with me. The first and last suggested that any type of relationship with the opposite sex was highly unlikely, and the other seemed to guarantee a relationship with the opposite sex but also came with a side of pregnancy topped with a butt whipping and an express ticket to hell. For these reasons, I steered clear of the three seeming demons for as long as I could withstand. As might be expected, one of the three—sex—was a bit more enticing than the others.

The verdict is still out on my trip to hell, but I avoided the dreaded butt whipping, as pregnancy did not come until I was twenty-nine and had earned a PhD. Yet, like many Black girls growing up in impoverished neighborhoods, I experienced sex at a young age—no talk, no understanding, no power, just looking to see what the fuss was all about. There was nearly a decade between my first sexual experience and my *conversion* to feminism, and while it has proven to be just as fussy as sex, feminism, most importantly, has provided me with a lens through which to examine my complicated relationships with other individuals, both sexually and nonsexually. It was the talk that I desperately needed during girlhood; it is the talk that I need now. Ultimately, feminism has enlightened me on the multifaceted world of human relations and has assisted me in recovering power I never knew that I had. But like me, Black feminism is also flawed.

I am cognizant that many girls and women, like my younger self, have never been encouraged to discuss and explore their sexualities, have relinquished or never knew that they had power, and are under the impression that feminism comes in a particular kind of packaging. It is my desire that this book will speak to women in both the streets and the academy and offer hope concerning the growing divide between scholars and the communities we theorize about. Essentially, I hope that the work of *maverick feminism* will dispel the myths concerning feminism and Black womanhood and give girls and women the language and tools to live out their truths, reclaim their everything, and get funky, thereby improving their own lives and the lives of the people around them.

WHAT IS MAVERICK FEMINISM?

The genesis of *maverick feminism* is grounded in a single question first posed by the father of the Harlem Renaissance, Alain Locke, in 1938 and later echoed by author and critic Nick Chiles in 2006: "But when will the Negro novelist of maturity, who knows how to tell a story convincingly . . . come to grips with motive fiction and social document fiction?" During the Harlem Renaissance, there were two schools of thought: that of the Black bourgeoisie and that of those described by Zora Neale Hurston as the *Niggerati*, a portmanteau of the terms *nigger* and *literati*. The self-proclaimed Niggerati, consisting of Hurston, Wallace Thurman, Langston Hughes, and other young, Black intellectuals who rejected respectability politics, prioritized folk culture, and sought individual joy, found itself in opposition to the Black bourgeoisie—older, middle-class, Black intellectuals, including Locke, who prioritized respectability, social equality, and racial integration. Locke's question is a manifestation of the groups' differences, as it is a direct response to Hurston's seminal text, *Their Eyes Were Watching God* (1937), and prioritizes racial propaganda over all else, particularly Black female sexualities. Locke and his contemporaries demeaned explicit sexuality and mistook or ignored the significant roles self-identification and self-sexualization played in the development of an individual, a community, and a race. Instead, they added sparks to the fire in the battle between popular and literary fiction. Maverick feminism, however, offers a means to settle the feud and bridge the gap between *highbrow* and *lowbrow* as it suggests that the terms are antiquated and that the personal or popular can, likewise, be sociopolitical. Fundamentally, the popular fiction novels analyzed in this text are not merely plot-driven entertainers; they, too, hold a mirror up to society and provide social commentary and political criticism.

The lens I use to evaluate the selected texts is called *maverick feminism*. Maverick feminism is not a new type of Black feminism; instead, it is an umbrella term comprising deviant Black feminisms such as that envisioned by Joan Morgan as well as those envisioned by radical feminists such as Audre Lorde, Alice Walker, Toni Cade Bambara, Barbara Smith, Gwendolyn Pough, and the Crunk Feminist Collective (CFC). These types of feminisms, whether declared lesbian feminism, womanism, Hip Hop feminism, crunk feminism, or something else, are forms of maverick feminism, contingent on independent thinking by women who do not conform to accepted views but who are dedicated to the initial principles of Black feminism as outlined in Patricia Hill Collins's *Black Feminist Thought* (1998): resisting and obliterating the oppression of racism, sexism, and classism; maintaining a humanist vision that will reject any human oppression; defining ourselves and speaking for those common Black women who may be voiceless; and finally, operating from a standpoint that acknowledges that the Black female experience is not monolithic, homogeneous, or uniform (18–19). Additionally, however, the primary tenant of maverick feminism is the belief that a person must become *self-identified, self-sexualized,* and *self-actualized* before one can wholly and successfully participate in the obliteration of racist, sexist, classist, and ableist oppressions enacted on others.

In "Scratching the Surface: Some Notes on Barriers to Women and Loving" (1978), Audre Lorde insists that self-identified Black women are "ready to explore and pursue our power and interests within our communities" and that it is "through the coming together of self-actualized individuals, female and male, that any real advances can be made." Lorde, too, suggests, "The old sexual power relationships based on a dominant/subordinate model between unequals have not served us as a people, nor as individuals (46). It is from this ideology, this shared belief, that I draw the key principles of maverick feminism: *self-identification, self-sexualization,* and *self-actualization.* Specifically, a person who is self-identified decides who they are and who they want to become without being swayed by parental, religious, or societal expectations. In a similar manner, being self-sexualized consists of not allowing others' perceptions of, or mandates for, "suitable" sexual behavior to limit or determine one's sexual desires or experiences, but rather the focus is on being a knowledgeable and active agent in one's intimate and sexual affairs (whether copious or nonexistent) while simultaneously being aware of the pleasures and consequences these affairs may present. Finally, self-actualization is but the ability to be unapologetic, bold, and accepting of one's newly carved identity. It is, essentially, the sum of being self-identified and self-sexualized.

The development of these characteristics is not an innate trait entrenched in all Black women, or all Black feminists for that matter. They are learned and taught traits, either through experiences of trauma—those that force Black women to peripheral positions beyond that of the natural subjugation intrinsically assigned to their race and gender, causing them to acknowledge that respectability does not guarantee respect—or positive connections with communities of already learned Black women. Maverick feminism acknowledges the role that psychology and mental health therapy, or the lack thereof, plays in helping Black women, and African Americans in general, become whole, healed, conscious beings but also recognizes that African Americans are less likely than other racial groups (particularly white Americans) to seek professional help for mental issues and, therefore, find other coping mechanisms. While the communal healing practices of maverick feminism, indeed, are an effective alternative, as they rely on a form of therapy detached from traditional, suppressive systems of medicine and psychology, it is my hope that maverick feminism will be taught, sought, and practiced by individuals before trauma is experienced, that it is practiced proactively as opposed to reactively. This theory posits an intergenerational method reminiscent of Angela Davis's "lift as we climb" theory and, therefore, acknowledges that one individual's ascension toward empowerment should result in the ascension of many others. The goal is to enlighten and embolden others in hopes of shielding them from physical and mental attacks—those from bigoted systems of oppression as well as those from individual tyrants—and to ultimately improve the systems that impact the well-being of Black women, men, and other individuals of marginalized communities.

In addition to the key principles of self-identification, self-sexualization, and self-actualization, maverick feminists also acknowledge and practice the following beliefs:

1. There is no singular Black womanhood.
2. Many women appreciate and even yearn for sexual attention.
3. There is power in critical discussion.
4. There is no power structure that is above critique.
5. The changing world is not to be feared.
6. The burden of representation does not rest on the shoulders of one individual.
7. Sisterhood promotes safety, sanity, sensuality, and success.

Ultimately, maverick feminism provides a freer, specifically more liberatory and less circumscribed, means of living out, evaluating, understanding, and improving the lives of Black women.

I am aware that the term *maverick* originated from, and is often associated with, white men; however, the term is defined simply as one who behaves or thinks independently. Essentially, a maverick is a nonconformist. History indicates that since America's supposed "founding," white men have often made the rules and therefore possessed fewer reasons to break them. People of color, however, Black women especially, since their forced advent on American soil, have exhibited maverick-like characteristics in order to survive and maintain a sense of semblance. I use this term, therefore, to celebrate centuries of agency and control that Black women have mustered and maintained in a world that seems to want nothing more than to see us prone and powerless. More precisely, I envision maverick feminism as a praxis specifically for/of Black or African American women. Allies of other sexes and races, however, may possess some maverick feminist characteristics, traits that they employ to help mobilize and sustain Black women's maverick feminism.

WHY ARE WE STILL TRYING TO MOVE BEYOND RESPECTABILITY POLITICS?

Echoing Audre Lorde's sentiments on self-definition, Toni Morrison, in *Beloved* (1987), her harrowing depiction of slavery and its aftermath, articulates the dynamics of power by insisting that "definitions belonged to the definers, not the defined" (190). Voyagers' attempts at defining the Black race predate the American institution of chattel slavery; therefore, the concepts of belonging and defining have always taken precedence in African American identities. In fact, Ta-Nehisi Coates exclaims that the Black body has never been in full ownership of the soul transporting it on a daily basis, that the pain or pleasure that it endures relies heavily on those in power, specifically individuals who "believe themselves to be white" (97). Acceptance of this lack of ownership prompted many African Americans to deny the body altogether, and deliberating over the body, particularly in terms of pleasure or sensual fulfillment, became a taboo that is still generally frowned on today.

Although not the first to do so, in 1991, the Black female rap group Salt-N-Pepa, eager to explore their sexualities and done skirting around the topic, issued a challenge to their audience, African Americans who had seemingly accepted bodily disenfranchisement: "Let's talk about sex . . . It keeps coming up anyhow / Don't decoy, avoid, or make void the topic / Cuz that aint gonna stop it . . . Let's tell it like it is, and how it could be / How it was, and of course, how it should be . . ." Indeed, the topic keeps coming up, and oftentimes in the most unlikely places. Whether former president Donald Trump is grabbing someone by the pussy, Jill Scott is simulating fellatio on her microphone, or Serena Williams is being slut-shamed for wearing a catsuit in a tennis match, allusions to gender and sexuality are inescapable. Of course, the attempted evasion of these vital discussions is due in part to the fact that for quite some time, the sexual composition and practices of the Black race, women in particular, gave individuals of other races reason to write home.

Richard Ligon is one notable European traveler who depicted the intimate lives of Africans during the mid-seventeenth century. He set sail from London and landed on the island of Barbados in 1647 with a goal of finding bounteous fruit and fertile land favorable for housing a sugar plantation. However, also principal to his *True and Exact History of the Island of Barbados* (1657) is the depiction of African women who, like their surroundings, appeared to be equally firm, fruitful, and sweet. On the other hand, Amerigo Vespucci's recount of his voyage through coastal Africa nearly 150 years earlier depicts the Black female body as both desirable and repulsive, while Robert Gainsh demonstrates little appreciation for the African women whom he encountered in Guinea and other equatorial regions on his 1554 voyage, describing the women using terms such as "rough," "savage," "wild," and "wondering," and noting that they had no *respect* for chastity.[3]

It is obvious that these travelers were unfamiliar with the practices and customs of the Africans they were encountering for the first time; they each seemed amazed even in their respective antipathy. And as is often true of the Western gaze, the travel writers' eyes became the lens through which many Europeans viewed Africans. In today's social media landscape, the travelogues, specifically depictions of first encounters with Africans, would be considered a viral sensation, as they spread all over the world with little to no concern with veracity or context. Ultimately, these men, sixteenth- and seventeenth-century travel writers, penned accounts of voyages and experiences with such confidence and conviction that Africans and African Americans, too, began to believe the pictures of themselves that others had drawn for them. It is as if Black men and women posed for a caricature and, not having access to a mirror of their own, misinterpreted the distorted figure as fact. The Black body was deduced to enlarged breasts and penises, insatiable sexual desires, rough and violent hands, wild and bewildering eyes, and strong and sturdy backs. Of course, as the "definers," Europeans became benefactors of the viral sensation, as their elaborate depictions of Africans gave support to their desires to enslave and tame said Africans, to rape and impregnate them, to silence and marginalize them, to misrepresent and misguide them, for over two hundred years. However, I argue that while the voyeurism of English travelers incited the initial oppression and brought light to the seemingly "shameful" sexual practices of African men and women, this shamefulness caused a repression of and violence against Black female sexuality that is oftentimes self-inflicted via respectability politics and/or toxic masculinity.

In addition to the sexual violence and physical damage to bodies, the separation of families, and the lack of financial self-sufficiency, among other injustices caused by the institution of slavery, the psyche of the Black race was severely wounded. Particularly, in the decades immediately after slavery was abolished, many Black women felt naked, permanently disrobed, visible for all to judge, reproach, and even devour, so there is no surprise that they attempted damage control and felt permanently on the defense. Candice M. Jenkins, in *Private Lives, Proper Relations: Regulating Black Intimacy* (2007), acknowledges that sexuality and intimacy are inherently political and insists that sexual silences and suppressions among African Americans was an attempt to "not only *be* full citizens, but to be *understood* as such" (4). I argue, however, that individuals concerned with repairing the image of the race failed to consider the fact that the definition "belonged" to the definer. In other words, it was not the defined's responsibility to carry the baggage. Understandably, early proponents of respectability politics did not have the foresight to see that forcing such practices on a community of already downtrodden and heavy-laden people to appease the unappeasable would have more penalties than rewards. Thus, many made attempts at eradicating anything and everything that remotely supported the definer's definition, thereby further marginalizing members of the very race they were attempting to pull from the said abyss.

For instance, during one of the most crucial times in Black history—the civil rights era—overtly sexual and "inappropriate" Black women were restricted from making significant contributions to the movement. More "respectful" Black women were recruited instead. Specifically, in March 1955, fifteen-year-old Claudette Colvin refused to give up her seat on a Montgomery bus because she felt that she was treated unjustly. Colvin was arrested and taken to jail, and her case eventually went to trial. Colvin's case was supposed to be used by the National Association for the Advancement of Colored People (NAACP) as the test case for civil rights, but because she was "unruly" during her arrest, "dragged from her seat by two men kicking and screaming . . . Black leaders and ordinary folks described Colvin as 'mouthy,' 'emotional,' and 'feisty'" (Harris 113). The later discovery that she was pregnant out of wedlock by a man thought to be married and white only compounded her inappropriateness, so Rosa Parks's case was used instead. Rather than becoming a famous civil rights hero, Colvin was charged with disorderly conduct, and her life story faded into the margins; she became someone's biological mother while Rosa Parks became known as the mother of the civil rights movement. Decades later, Colvin reflects on her rejection, questioning, "I knew they couldn't put me on stage like the queen of the boycott, but after what I had done, why did they have to turn their backs on me?" (Hoose 105). Fredrick C. Harris agrees that the community's rejection of Colvin was murky, stating, "The call for this type of upright moral behavior was more a strategy to legitimize nonviolent resistance than an appeal to whites to accept blacks on equal terms because of their proven moral worth" (113). Besides, many African Americans themselves failed to see their own moral worth.

In the late nineteenth century, elite Black women began to formulate clubs in support of political issues such as women's suffrage and antilynching reform, and in 1895, members of these clubs gathered at the First National Conference of the Colored Women of America with the purpose of forming a national organization. From this organization sprang forth many others, specifically the Woman's Convention, which was materialized in 1900 as an auxiliary to the National Baptist Convention. It is indeed risky to mix politics and religion, but Black churches have seldom shied away from this endeavor; it often serves as a safe haven for political figures hoping to escape their enemies but subsequently becomes a deathbed for unsuspecting parishioners, such as the four little girls of the 16th Street Baptist Church in Birmingham, Alabama, (1963) and the nine individuals who lost their lives during the massacre at Emanuel African Methodist Episcopal Church in Charleston, South Carolina (2015). Not all Black church massacres have been carried out by white supremacists, however, and not all of the massacres have been physical in nature.

In her seminal work, *Righteous Discontent: The Women's Movement in the Black Baptist Church* (1993), Evelyn Brooks Higginbotham illustrates the debilitating effects of social massacres by providing a thorough outline and analysis of the women's movement and ultimately demonstrates how Black Baptist women themselves supported supremacist ideologies under the guise of reforming and transforming the nation. Higginbotham suggests that the Woman's Convention "afforded black women what Patricia Hill Collins calls a 'safe space' for self-definition. The vast crowds who flocked to the WC's annual assemblies stirred feelings of freedom and security. In these assemblies black Baptist women expressed themselves openly and without fear of reprisal" (186). The problem, I argue, is that their *self*-definitions were not self-fulfilling; they were simply blatant refutations of the definitions of European travelers, white slave owners, and the general public who had bought into the caricatures sketched by their predecessors. Possessing safe spaces of their own also seemed to be dependent on ascertaining that their neighbors' spaces were less free. For these Black women, "the politics of respectability emphasized reform of individual behavior and attitudes both as a goal in itself and as a strategy for reform of the entire structural system of American race relations" (Higginbotham 187). Members of the organization, recognized by themselves and others as members of the Talented Tenth, disseminated literature, opened schools, hosted conventions, and gave speeches in the hopes of "lifting up the race," meeting the status quo, and gaining the respect of tyrants.

Both Evelyn Brooks Higginbotham and Fredrick C. Harris acknowledge that the Black Baptist women of the Woman's Convention thought of themselves as exemplars for the poor and wicked of their race who needed "special instructions" (Harris 105). They possessed what Candice Jenkins (2002) calls the *salvific wish*, "an aspiration, most often but not only middle-class and female, to save or rescue the black community from white racist accusations of sexual and domestic pathology, through the embrace of conventional bourgeois propriety" (973). Higginbotham urges that "the WC's enormous concern for whites' perception of black behavior regularly prompted scathing critiques against nonconformity to 'proper values'" (194). This idea of conformity is one of absurdity, especially coming from a group of women supposedly beholden to spaces of self-definition, because, inherently, the WC "reinforced prevalent stereotypical images of blacks" and charged the Black poor with solving America's problems (194). Young girls in particular were scolded because they were thought to "go in pairs or in shoals, string themselves in a line across the sidewalk, making it almost impossible for others to pass . . . exceedingly boisterous in their conduct . . . patrol[ling] the streets until late in the night" (Higginbotham 199). Even more, the women insisted that the girls wore questionable clothes in gaudy colors and danced like animals that had made "a voluntary return to the jungle" (200). Ultimately, Black church women who so harshly judged and policed their counterparts unwittingly supported the very definitions they were trying to refute. As Joan Morgan notes, "Defining ourselves solely by our oppression denies us the very magic of who we are" (60). This denial of magic became a common trend among Black elites even beyond the women's movement and civil rights movement.

For instance, comedian Bill Cosby is known for many things; one of those things is his scathing 2004 attack on the Black poor. He acknowledges, "Ladies and gentlemen, the lower economic and lower middle economic people are not holding their end in this deal . . . Fifty percent drop-out rate, I'm telling you, and people in jail, and women having children by five, six different men . . . Under what excuse," he questions. His response to the question is fervently condescending: "I want somebody to love me. And as soon as you have it, you forget to parent. Grandmother, mother, and great-grandmother in the same room, raising children, and the child knows nothing about love or respect of any one of the three of them," he insists (Harris 119–20). Cosby assumed he had the right to condemn others because he married and bore children with a presumably wholesome Black woman, used comedy to work his way into the hearts and homes of Americans, was awarded a doctoral degree, and grossed millions of dollars as an actor and producer. Seemingly, he had "held his end in the deal" by being respectable. Interestingly enough, he seemed to have forgotten that he, too, dropped out of high school, and even more, he, very recently, was one of those "people in jail," accused of committing sex crimes against more than fifty women. Under what excuse, I ask? . . . So much for the deal.

To be clear, supporting or negating respectability politics is not a matter of good versus evil or nonsexual versus sexual. A person can reject respectability politics and still choose to live a moderately sexual life or even a life devoid of sex altogether. This person must be self-sexualized though. As stated previously, a self-sexualized individual is one who does not allow others' perceptions of, or mandates for, "suitable" sexual behavior to limit or determine one's sexual desires or experiences, but rather the focus is on being a knowledgeable and active agent in one's intimate and sexual affairs, whether nonexistent or copious. Among all the other problems with respectability politics is the precise ordeal of imperfect people policing and chastising imperfect people, all to gain the respect of imperfect people— elitism at its finest. For this reason, this study shifts the terms of the debate from considerations of respectability as a judgment tool to examining, alternatively, the impact of Black women who ignore the definer's definition, even when the definer is a member of their own communities. More specifically, this study examines the impact of women who use their lived experiences and unapologetic sexualities to affect positive change by promoting self-exploration and self-care, practices that in turn result in communal wellness and growth.

HOW DOES RESPECTABILITY LIMIT BLACK
LITERATURE AND ACTIVISM?

Noting the often limited and one-dimensional depictions of African American women in literary, political, and scholarly arenas, Joan Morgan insists:

> Discovering the works of Alice Walker, Angela Davis, Audre Lorde, Paula Giddings, and bell hooks—black women who claimed the f-word boldly—not only enabled me to understand the complex and often explicit relationship between both isms [sexism and racism]; it empowered me with language to express the unique oppression that comes with being colored and a woman. I was eternally grateful, but I was not a feminist. (37)

Like me before I was introduced to her work, Morgan was not yet a feminist because, to her, feminism seemed to be yet another restricting system designed to deny the Black body pleasure and joy; specifically, her concern was that it focused too much on the oppression of the Black female body and not enough on its freedoms and desires. This type of feminism, therefore, did not cater to her generation, everyday women who were the product of a Hip Hop movement that was unapologetic in its exploration of race, class, and gender politics.

Historically, Black women artists who centralized pleasure, or real-life women like Claudette Colvin who *seemed* to have centralized pleasure, were marginalized and often "lost" altogether.[4] For instance, in her groundbreaking work titled *Black Women Novelists: The Development of a Tradition, 1892–1976* (1980), Black feminist literary critic Barbara Christian maps out the literary tradition of Black women novelists by examining its origins, tracing the development of stereotypes of Black women, and evaluating the effect those stereotypes had on literature written by Black women. Christian acknowledges Frances E. W. Harper's *Iola Leroy* (1892) as the first novel published by an African American woman. In 1982, however, only two years after the publication of Christian's work, scholar Henry Louis Gates Jr. dug a little deeper into the margins, rediscovered Harriet Wilson's *Our Nig; or, Sketches from the Life of a Free Black, in a Two-Story White House, North* (1859), and determined that not only was it the first novel published by an African American woman, but it was the first novel—despite arguably autobiographical features—published by an African American in general. The omission and marginalization of Wilson's contribution, like that of Colvin's, may not have been a deliberate attempt at revisionist history, but it definitely aligns with deliberate attempts to marginalize the Black female body, denying it pleasure, and refusing to see it as subject. Perhaps it more aptly characterizes what I would call *divisionist history*, or dividing historical truths into sections with hopes that the least favorable aspects will fade into the margins.

Interestingly, through the mulatto characters of Iola and Frado, respectively, both *Iola Leroy* and *Our Nig* served as a refutation of negative Black female images and a critique of wavering abolitionists and interracial marriage, but Wilson's work, as it was published anonymously, was a bit more explicit in its critique. For instance, Frado is an everyday woman known for her "jollity" and enjoyment of life's simple *pleasures*; she questions religion and nearly all manner of authority. Iola Leroy, on the other hand, accepts a proposal from and marries Dr. Latimer, not for the sake of love or intimacy or any personal longing, but for a shared concern for the race and obedience to religious expectations. Essentially, Frado, aligning more with contemporary feminists, is deviant, while Iola Leroy is the portrait of a "respectable" woman. Consequently, although the field of African American literature was mostly populated by male writers for quite some time after the publication of Harper's novel in 1892, the example set forth in *Iola Leroy*, of repressing a deviant sexuality in return for a more respectable lifestyle, was followed by a great many Black women novelists.

As a result, the trajectory of the depiction of Black female sexualities by Black women writers from the late nineteenth century to the early twenty-first century is as follows: first, during the turn of the twentieth century, Black women writers attempted to refute and counteract negative societal images by creating Black women characters that were asexual, usually mulatto, civil, and respected. Harlem Renaissance writers depicted a different class of Black female characters that relished Black (folk) culture and were covertly sexual. This characterization was followed by the 1950s and '60s illustration of the ordinary Black woman character that, although somewhat sexual, was seldom desired or respected because of her class. Later, the women of the 1970s created Black female characters that acknowledged the past but attempted to make their own rules regarding sexuality and Black womanhood. Finally, contemporary Black women novelists, having the luxury of ignoring history and its negative images, are beginning to tell their own personal or sexual tales by creating Black female characters similar to themselves, attempting to survive in late twentieth- and early twenty-first-century societies. In sum, as a result of the example set by Harper and the continued desires for respectability, despite a 160-plus-year history of African American women's novels, only within the past few decades, with the exception of a few deviant artists, has the Black woman's novel been centered around an unapologetically sexual female character that places her own desires before those of others.

In *Beyond Respectability: The Intellectual Thought of Race Women* (2018), Brittney Cooper asks readers to "consider what Black women thinkers said about Black women's lives, and Black possibility, beyond the discourse of respectability," and she analyzes and interrogates the works of Mary Church Terrell, Fannie Barrier Williams, Pauli Murray, and Toni Cade Bambara, using a theory she calls embodied discourse.[5] *Maverick Feminist* extends this conversation to include Black women who are not often thought of as race women and works that not only demand that the Black female body not be ignored, but also unapologetically advocate for and signify the importance of the sexual fulfillment of the Black female body, as the works analyzed in this book suggest that one must first be self-identified, self-sexualized, and self-actualized before helping to reduce or eradicate the oppressions of others. In other words, I argue that when Black women are free and autonomous within themselves, they have the necessary experience and tools to help free others. Marginalized examples in literature and sensual explorations doused by respectability politics nearly annihilated this freedom; *Maverick Feminist* celebrates the tradition of feminists, writers, and politicians who refused to be deterred.

Freedom and activism come in many shapes and forms. Ultimately, to be an advocate is to use whatever platform or stage one has available to promote a cause that will positively affect a population that is often marginalized and/or discriminated against due to race, gender, class, ability, or any other categorization that might place one at a disadvantage in majority society. When sexual deviancy is added to the equation, or when one defies the politics of respectability, discriminatory acts, such as a lack of recognition in popular and academic sectors, increase exponentially. Yet the most effective Black women activists in history have often followed this tradition.

For instance, Angelina Weld Grimké is often chided for poetry that is too emotional and fiction that is too blunt; seemingly she was unapologetic in her loving as well as her loathing. And while it is mostly her abolitionist/antilynching work that receives recognition—perhaps because she lived what some would consider a "hidden" lesbian life and did not practice her sexuality boldly—I would argue that her lesbianism was hidden in plain sight and that she rejected respectability politics even when she seemed to have honored the system. Furthermore, she predicted that her life would have benefited greatly if she had been able to engage in a sisterhood, specifically an intergenerational relationship with a female elder who, like herself, might have been bold and deviant. Intergenerational relationships and sisterhoods do not require one to follow the leader or to worship others as "role models," as all are human, prone to failure, and therefore not ideal. However, these relationships offer the epistemology of an elder or more experienced, self-identified peer to help stimulate one's own self-definition and growth. Grimké writes in a diary entry, "I suppose I was a fool and oh how I wish that I had a mother!" (Herron 11).[6] Furthermore, in a poem "honoring" her father on his fifty-fifth birthday, she mostly honors his mother and conceives of him as an infant/child for the majority of the poem. She credits her life to him, including "all that is good" in her, and questions what she would be without his help. We can gather from her poems and letters that she might have been more open about her sexuality without "his help," which also means that she would have been, according to society, the opposite of good. She might have been happier, though, and her poems and fiction might have taken a less dark and sappy tone. Although Grimké's letters suggest that her lesbian affairs offered her some semblance of pleasure, a repressed sexuality and lack of female companion—as either mother or friend—ultimately manifested itself in her literature. She was devoid of what Morrison calls in *Beloved* a gatherer, or someone to take the pieces of her and give them back "in all the right order." In *Black Women, Identity, and Cultural Theory* (2004), Kevin Quashie, too, recognizes the healing power of sisterhood among Black women, stating, "The girlfriend is that other someone who makes it possible for a black female subject to bring more of herself into consideration, to imagine herself in a wild safety. A woman is encouraged by her girlfriend to be herself radically, even as the heft of doing so might be too much for the connection to bear" (18). Grimké lacked the pleasure of a wild safety, but her life and works stand as testament to its significance.

On the contrary, Fannie Lou Hamer was robbed of her opportunity to mother, and few would willingly align her with other feminist activists, specifically because she blatantly rejected its principles on several occasions, but also because, as is the case with Grimké, we like to practice *divisionist history* and center Hamer's legacy on race relations alone. Nonetheless, she often used the platform she gained from her voters' rights work to protest against the injustices of the 1964 sterilization bill, a law insisting that "if a woman had one illegitimate child and then a second one, they could draw time for 6 months or a $500 fine." She notes in response, "What they didn't tell is that they are already doing these things [sterilizing women], not only to single women but to married women" (C. K. Lee 80). Hamer knew from experience that this deed was likewise enacted on married women because she was forced to undergo this very sterilization after being admitted into the hospital to have a cyst removed. Presumably, the doctors determined that the African American offspring/population itself was a cyst infecting the well-being of American society, and Hamer devoted the remainder of her life to negating such stereotypes.

Unfortunately, while returning from a trip to South Carolina, where she was attempting to fulfill this mission, she was subjected to physical and sexual violence in a Winona, Mississippi, jail. She remembers the patrolman's constant attempt to feel under her clothes as she fought vigorously to pull down her dress. She was not just a Black activist; she knew as well as the policemen that her gender and sexuality were always present and up front, so much so that during a 1971 speech in which she seemingly rejects feminism, Hamer insists:

And you know, I'm not hung up on this liberating myself from the black man, I'm not going to try that thing. I got a black husband, six feet three, two hundred and forty pounds, with a 14 shoe, that I don't want to be liberated from. But we are here to work side by side with this black man in trying to bring liberation to all people.

I suppose that Hamer rejected feminism for the same reason that I initially rejected it, thinking that there was only one way to be a (Black) feminist. Black feminism was still restricted by respectability politics, and unapologetic sexualities were not yet affirmed. Hamer's bold determination to both express her sexuality and fight the world with her "six feet three, two hundred and forty pounds, [size] 14 shoe" husband is more akin to contemporary feminists' commitments to their causes and their husbands (e.g., the Obamas, the Carters even) and is essential to this study as Hamer is the first of many Black women who seemingly understands the fact that pleasure for one can result in progress for many. L. H. Stallings (2015) insists, "Fucking has always been leisure activity with functional and aesthetic value, but it was civilization and then modernity's manifest destiny that tasked it with nation building and made it into a labor-intensive model of production and reproduction" (35). Perhaps we would prefer not to think of the incomparable Fannie Lou Hamer in such a sexual manner, but I would argue that Hamer is one of the few who got it right. Her lack of ability to reproduce did not diminish her desires for pleasure with her robust and well-endowed husband, and her desires for pleasure did not diminish her impact on society.

Fannie Lou Hamer and Marsha P. Johnson could not be more different, yet they are so much alike. Born Malcolm Michaels Jr. to parents who did not support her identity as a homosexual, Johnson insisted that the *P* in the new name she gave herself stood for "Pay it no mind," yet she devoted and arguably gave her life so that gay and trans communities would be heavily on the minds of American society.[7] In 2018, the *New York Times* recognized the conundrums resulting from intentional marginalization and divisionist history and created an obituary section titled "Overlooked," where it narrated the life and death of women, mostly women of color, whose art or deeds had prominently affected society but had garnered little to no recognition upon their deaths. Johnson is heralded as "an activist, a prostitute, a drag performer, and, for nearly three decades, a fixture of street life in Greenwich Village." In addition to these "accolades," she battled mental illness, poverty, and homelessness. She is definitely not the poster child for respectability, but her fight and struggles, specifically with mental illness, are realities that African Americans cannot ignore. Strength is both a gift and a curse, even more so in Black communities where seeking psychological counsel is often thought of as a weakness. Johnson's life is a testament to the fact that taking the necessary measures to ensure one's own sanity and joy, especially sexually, is the epitome of bravery and strength. [8]

Each of these women/activists shared their lives and stories as sexual and societal deviants, displayed characteristics akin to maverick feminism, and as a result did not receive their just due. They are not the most acclaimed women in (African) American history, but the impact they have/had on gender politics in America is undeniable. They make space for and centralize the stories of women of color who do not fit society's mold and suggest to everyday women that feminism can play a role in their lives. Finally, they acknowledge that freedom, and therefore joy, are rarely obtained by doing things "the usual way." Their nonconformist, individualistic, yet community-centric ideologies are what steered me in the direction of feminism and are the bedrock of maverick feminism, the lens through which I analyze the works in this book.

WHY THE FOCUS ON SEXUALITY?

Sixteenth-century travel writers. Antebellum South slave owners. Thomas Jefferson. The Ku Klux Klan. Clarence Thomas. Bill Cosby. Robert Kelly. Harvey Weinstein. Donald Trump. Gender, sex, and sexuality have always held prominence in the underbelly of American society. The abovementioned men and organizations can be recognized by individuals from all walks of life in households all over the country. The women they trampled over, however, are often nameless or forgotten, considered victims and objects, hardly ever survivors or subjects. In this project, I evaluate the lives and sexualities of Black women beyond their victimhood and offer unapologetic exploration of one's own passions and pleasures as a means for both individual and communal progression.

Evelynn Hammonds, over two and a half decades ago, recognized a lack of scholarship exploring the pleasurable, healing aspects of Black female sexualities, and in an essay titled "Black (W)holes and the Geometry of Black Female Sexuality" (1994) insists:

> The restrictive, repressive, and dangerous aspects of female sexuality have been emphasized by black feminist writers, while pleasure, exploration, and agency have gone under-examined . . . Reclaiming the body as well as subjectivity is a process that black feminist theorists in the academy must go through themselves while they are doing the work of producing theory. (99)

Hammonds suggests that writing about Black women and their bodies is only half the battle, that Black feminists themselves must reclaim and explore their own bodies in the process. In other words, she urges scholars to "go there to know there," just as I argue that one must be self-identified, self-sexualized, and self-actualized before aiding in the emancipation of others.

Instead of scholars focusing their attention on the emancipation of others, however, Fredrick Harris notes that researchers and writers have been influential in reviving respectability politics, which after being denounced by Black Power supporters of the 1970s, resurfaced in the late 1980s as a direct defense against unapologetic explorations of issues such as sexuality, poverty, race, and violence. Harris notes:

> By the late 1980s, and certainly by the 1990s, the politics of respectability began to reemerge. Its reemergence was brought about by two similar but separate discourses in the academy and media—the appearance of a so-called urban underclass and the rise of gangsta rap. While structural explanations had been the dominant academic approach to explicate the plight of the black poor since the 1960s, newspaper articles, magazine

stories, television documentaries, and academic studies began
to report that the values of the black poor were different than
the rest of society. The black poor were portrayed as embracing
self-destructive values that kept them entrapped in poverty.
And in addition to the social isolation that the black poor experience, they—especially poor black youth—were thought to
be embracing a destructive culture that promoted antisocial
and deviant behavior. (116)

Unfortunately, scholars bought into the bootstrap model that suggested that if members of poor Black communities refrained from
listening to gangsta rap and subsequently stopped being delinquents
who abused drugs, alcohol, and sex, their problems would be solved.
However, Patricia Hill Collins, in her groundbreaking work, *Black
Sexual Politics* (2005), immediately rejects this idealism and insists
that emancipation requires us as a nation to first accept the fact that
a great majority of the country's issues are directly linked to gender
and sexuality, that the issues that have been marginalized and pushed
to the underbelly of society are in fact more central than we would
like to concede. She argues:

> Poverty, unemployment, rape, HIV/AIDS, incarceration, sub-
> stance abuse, adolescent pregnancy, high rates of Black chil-
> dren in foster care, intraracial violence (especially by young
> Black males as both victims and perpetrators), and similar
> issues have a disproportionate impact on African Americans.
> All of these social problems take gender-specific forms, and
> none will be solved without serious attention to the politics
> of gender and sexuality. Black women can never become fully
> empowered in a context that harms Black men, and Black men
> can never become fully empowered in a society in which Black
> women cannot fully flourish as human beings. (7)

Even more, she recognizes that the Black church, on account of respectability politics, is more of a hindrance than a solution in the
areas of gender and sexuality in particular, stating, "Black Christian
churches constitute the most important African American community

organizations, and yet they continue to preach a conservative gender ideology, and shun controversial topics, especially sexuality" (45). Of course, because so many scholars themselves are middle-class individuals subscribing to the doctrine of the church and respectability, delving deeply into the world of female sexualities and pleasures is often an antagonistic venture, one that Stacey Patton outlines in her critical work "Who's Afraid of Black Sexualities?" (2012).

Patton argues that Black scholars and African Americans in general have been afraid to discuss Black sexualities openly and critically because the conversations would conjure up too many stereotypes. Quite frankly, the conversations will conjure up the caricatures drawn by travel writers in the sixteenth and seventeenth centuries, stereotypes transfixed into minds of enslaved people and slave owners and perpetuated by contemporary white supremacists. Even young girls are fearful of these stereotypes, afraid that any exploration or appreciation of their own bodies and sexualities will thwart their potential to be treated with respect or to thrive in this country. Shayne Lee, in *Erotic Revolutionaries* (2010), insists that popular culture figures who are often the leaders and precursors of trends, particularly trends that scholars theorize about, "defile traditional prescriptions for female prudence and inaugurate sexual scripts that carve new spaces for eroticism and sexual freedom" (128). So many young girls and women, though, are still afraid, literally, to follow such scripts.

Because she identified as a feminist in her 2013 self-titled album and is heralded as the queen of pop—two seemingly different worlds, Beyoncé studies have abounded in the past decade. Books, journal articles, think pieces, and syllabi proudly don the name of the Queen Bey. However, in a study conducted in 2017 titled "What Does Beyoncé Mean to Young Girls?," Ebony Utley made the most intriguing discovery. Utley found that young girls ages eleven to sixteen generally admired Beyoncé but refused to see her as a "role model," primarily because they were afraid that adopting Beyoncé's unapologetic ways of expressing sexuality increased their "vulnerability to the negative stereotypes of people who do not know them but have derogatory perceptions of the neighborhood from which they hail" (7). In other words, they were afraid that exuding Beyoncé-like confidence, though empowering and self-satisfying, would make them targets of unfair and violent treatment from others. They were afraid to explore and appreciate their own identities for fear that their newfound visibility would invite others to violate them. Essentially, young girls and women are afraid to be subjects with agency for fear that it will result in their objectification and victimhood. Sadly, they are afraid to live for fear that they might die. And this is why female sexualities, specifically those of marginalized women of color, require more thorough exploration.

Joan Morgan insists that we provide a space where damaged or traumatized sexualities do not take center stage, a space for "honest bodies that like also to fuck," and conduct a necessary *renovation* of Black feminist thought that "encourages recognition of black women's pleasure (sexual and otherwise) as not only an integral part of fully realized humanity, but one that understands that a politics of pleasure is capable of intersecting, challenging, and redefining dominant narratives about race, beauty, health, and sex in ways that are generative and necessary" ("Why We Get Off" 46). I offer maverick feminism as such a space to focus on the self who is attempting to move, or has moved, beyond the trauma and into a self-fulfilling environment that benefits entire communities. To be clear, I do not suggest that maverick feminism is some type of magic shield, that no harm or danger will come upon one once they have adopted the practice, or that it will automatically relieve ongoing trauma. Instead, again, it offers a freer, specifically more liberatory and less circumscribed, means of living out, evaluating, understanding, and improving the lives of Black women. Furthermore, the practice of maverick feminism is an acknowledgement that the more we teach Black girls and women to be unapologetically aware and possessive of their own bodies, the less power other people, particularly violent men and proponents of respectability politics, will have over them.

WHAT CAN READERS EXPECT FROM
THE REMAINING CHAPTERS?

In the tradition of Paula Giddings's *When and Where I Enter: The Impact of Black Women on Race and Sex in America* (1984), Trudier

Harris's *Saints, Sinners, and Saviors: Strong Black Women in African American Literature* (2002), and Brittney Cooper's *Beyond Respectability: The Intellectual Thought of Race Women* (2018), in this book, *Maverick Feminist,* I conduct a close reading of texts authored by and/ or about bold and *bad* Black women who positively impact American politics and culture. The Black women characters that I analyze use their sexualities as a means of self-improvement, activism, and communal growth. I find that these women often reject respectability politics and other conventions that tend to tame African Americans, specifically African American women, by limiting their personal satisfaction and joy, thereby pushing already marginalized groups even further into the margins.

Maverick Feminist also builds on the work of Kenneth Warren. In *What Was African American Literature* (2012), Warren argues that the impetus for and necessity of African American literature as a national literature no longer exists in the current day as the literature was developed during the Jim Crow era as a means to voice grievances against segregation and to promote equality among the races. Although *Maverick Feminist* does not claim to define African American literature or attempt to support or disprove Warren's theory, it does offer other separatist tactics (conventional or criminal) as means for African Americans to continue to produce and procure literature and other modern cultural productions as a form of protest and self-advancement. In other words, that specific battle may be over, but the war is not. Thus, this type of protest literature lives on, specifically in the actions, writings, and thoughts of Black women.

Echoing the concerns of her fellow pleasure ninja who ponders the reasons why "the gainfully degreed would rather trick away our last twenty-five dollars on that new nineties black girl fiction than some of those good, but let's face it, laboriously academic black feminist texts," Brittney Cooper insists in *Beyond Respectability,* "If we actually want to take Black women seriously as thinkers and knowledge producers, we must begin to look for their thinking in unexpected places, to expect its incursions in genres like autobiography, novels, news stories, medical records, organizational histories, public speeches, and diary entries (Morgan 53; Cooper 12). I carry this same sentiment and therefore call on the knowledge of Black women in many different genres, including novels, autobiographies, web television series, music videos, essays, speeches, and letters. More specifically, at the heart of each chapter, with the exception of chapter three, is a comparative analysis of two fictional works centering Black women's developing sexualities. These analyses highlight the importance of sisterhoods and intergenerational dynamics and are foregrounded and supported by popular culture productions. Finally, I end each chapter by examining a memoir penned by a Black woman who admittedly rejected respectability politics on account of its debilitating and joy-stifling potentials. The organization of each chapter serves as a direct response to Locke's question concerning Hurston's supposed misuse of a "cradle gift": the ability to be human, evoke the culture, and "tell a story convincingly"—specifically as opposed to allowing her character to "div[e] down deep either to the inner psychology of characterization or to sharp analysis of the social background." Ultimately, I contend that the separation of literature from lives is at the base of the false categorization dividing "serious" literature from popular texts as literary and cultural studies both affirm and improve the lives of Black women.

In the first chapter, "Dirty Computers: Girlhood and Sexual Desires," I argue that the very sexual protagonists in Zora Neale Hurston's *Their Eyes Were Watching God* (1937) and Sister Souljah's *The Coldest Winter Ever* (2000) attempt to operate as maverick feminists and are influential to the growth of other Black women as a direct result of their self-identified and/or self-sexualized mentalities. However, because both Janie and Winter operate in a society where an overt sexuality is seemingly punishable, the protagonists, like their authors, are banished to some form of imprisonment by the end of their respective narrative. Hence, while the works are undoubtedly groundbreaking, and the depictions of Black female sexualities portrayed in them add depth and diversity to the body of criticism on Black female sexualities, they are also, ultimately, representatives of the societal two-ness imposed on the Black female body during the sixteenth and seventeenth centuries. Cardi B.'s pronouncement on agency, respectability, and class, as vocalized in her song "I Do" (2018) foregrounds the chapter, and I offer Brittney Cooper's critical memoir, *Eloquent Rage: A Black Feminist Discovers Her Superpower*

(2018), as a final, nonfictional account of the debilitating impact of respectability politics.

The main characters analyzed in chapter two, "Be Careful with Me: Education, Sexual Violence, and Pleasure," are the exact opposites of those analyzed in chapter one, as Celie of Alice Walker's *The Color Purple* (1982) and Precious Jones of Sapphire's *PUSH* (1996) are not self-identified or self-sexualized and, early on, lack a desire for sexual pleasure. Both also lack education and are mentally, physically, and sexually abused by their respective father figure. This type of sexual trauma has often been a focal point in Black feminist thought. However, this chapter centralizes the fact that these characters are defined not by their trauma but by their sexual (r)evolutions. By the novels' ends, the protagonists are attached to communities of women that possess and help the characters develop necessary tools for freedom (namely self-identification, self-sexualization, and self-actualization)—a freedom that is taken away from the protagonists examined in the previous chapter. To further demonstrate the interconnectedness of sisterhood, sexuality, and progression, I also analyze the film versions of this chapter's two primary texts and determine that the novels' protagonists develop and become more complicated characters than their film counterparts as a direct result of their explicit, intimate experiences and engagements with others. Then, to provide a nonfictional representation of this dilemma, I offer Roxane Gay's memoir, *Hunger: A Memoir of (My) Body* (2017). Gay endured physical and sexual abuse and suffers from past and present "shames." Her work's acknowledgement of continued sufferings magnifies a purpose of chapter two, which is to illustrate that a sensual education is equally important to the overall well-being of African American women and girls as a conventional education.

Chapter three, "Get in Formation: Sisterhood and the Intergenerational Dynamic," serves as a representation of what is initially lacking in the lives of the main characters in chapters one and two. In chapter three, I conduct a close reading of Terry McMillan's *Getting to Happy* (2013) to articulate the ways in which an intentional sisterhood or intergenerational dynamic can personally fulfill the women involved while also propelling political and social agendas. The novel both revisits and reunites the four charismatic and driven women from *Waiting to Exhale*, but the general purpose of *Getting to Happy* is to express that "times have changed." To demonstrate these changing times and the need to be proactive, McMillan uses the outspoken and unapologetic offspring of the four protagonists to highlight the importance of reverencing one's past and understanding one's present in order to be productive and happy in one's future. Historically, young Black women have been compelled to think of other Black women as competition, and older Black women have often thought of the young as ill-informed or incapable of leading. However, McMillan's *Getting to Happy* demonstrates the reward in finding a common ground, or a space in the median where both entities can equally soar while working toward a common goal of alleviating oppressions. On the surface, this idea of the happy medium may appear too idealistic and seemingly unsophisticated, but ultimately this chapter is confirmation that the happy medium approach is undoubtedly more beneficial to and representative of the avant-garde, diverse, and continuously changing world in which we live, operate, and theorize. Finally, as in the previous two chapters, I call on the lived experiences of Black women to validate the claims depicted in the fictional works. *Red Table Talk*, a Facebook original web series starring Jada Pinkett Smith and her mother and daughter, foregrounds the chapter and demonstrates the power and evolution that result from tackling life's enterprises via critical, honest, and open dialogue with female companions. Michelle Obama's memoir *Becoming* also helps to dispel myths about respectability and supports the idea that participation in a sisterhood and/or intergenerational relationship is beneficial for all involved.

Finally, in the book's conclusion, I reflect on the importance of this work to the fields of Black feminist theory and literary and cultural studies. I reassert my central argument and offer suggestions for further research, staging my own reimagining of a Black feminist theory that more seriously engages everyday people and popular culture productions. I end with rumination on the magic that Black women have produced in a country that has never favored it and use this display of resilience as hope for a future where pleasure for all is the new standard.

Chapter One

DIRTY COMPUTER

Girlhood and Sexual Desires

Now, women forget all those things they don't want to remember and remember everything they don't want to forget. The
dream is the truth. Then they act and do things accordingly.
—ZORA NEALE HURSTON, *THEIR EYES WERE WATCHING GOD* (1937)

Progressive Black women authors allow their Black female characters to dream because they realize that the race's continued progress
depends on the fulfillment of dreams; they also acknowledge, as Joan
Morgan (2000) proclaims, "that there is no dream I can't pursue *and
achieve* simply because 'I am a woman'" (59; emphasis original). Miss
Universe 2019, South Africa's Zozibini Tunzi, joins in on this conversation, insisting that "the most important thing we should be teaching
young girls today is leadership." She continues by stating, "It's something that has been lacking in young girls and women for a long time,
not because we don't want to, but because of what society has labeled
women to be . . . we are the most powerful beings in the world . . .
and that is what we should be teaching these young girls, to take up
space." Tunzi insists, "Nothing is as important as taking up space in
society and cementing yourself" (ABS-CBN Entertainment). Notori-
ous female rapper Cardi B., too, acknowledges and is a testament to
the importance of taking up space and cementing oneself in society,
as she, in the same year that Tunzi was crowned, 2019, became the
first solo female artist to win a Grammy for Best Rap Album with her
debut album, *Invasion of Privacy*. In this album, she proclaims that
women and girls do not pursue many of their dreams because they
are restricted by respectability politics, because they are determined

to be "good girls." Similarly, Laurel Thatcher Ulrich, over five decades ago, insisted that "well-behaved women seldom make history," and this chapter adds that likewise, *good girls* are frequently lacking in joy, pleasure, and fulfillment. On the other hand, *bad girls* regularly realize these sensations but tend to find themselves ostracized from their communities as a result. Though *bad* and *sexually active* are not synonymous and *respectability* and *goodness* are, likewise, not synonymous, as Higginbotham acknowledges that the church women practiced righteous discontent as a form of social and political activism, the female characters analyzed in this chapter are deemed "bad" because they do not follow their community's accepted norms, including how they practice their sexuality. But the protagonists in Zora Neale Hurston's *Their Eyes Were Watching God* and Sister Souljah's *The Coldest Winter Ever*, intriguingly, use these moments of isolation to find themselves, define themselves, and offer their own experiences as means to question or dismantle systems of oppression, thereby empowering others, oftentimes the very individuals and communities who isolated them.

HOT GIRL SUMMER:
JANIE'S JOURNEY TO MARRIAGE

Over the past few years, as sexual explicitness and sexual exploitation have become more widely addressed in mass media and everyday life, contemporary scholars have become more engaged with sexualities studies, emphasizing the connection between the academy and everyday life that is often forgotten. A number of anthologies on Black sexualities have been published in the past decade and a half, including *Black Sexualities: Probing Powers, Passions, Practices, and Policies* (2009) edited by Juan Battle and Sandra Barnes and *Black Female Sexualities* (2015) edited by Trimiko Melancon and Joanne Braxton. Essays and articles on the topic have also been impactful. Specifically, Stacey Patton (2012), in a probing essay in the *Chronicle of Higher Education*, deduced scholars' and society's general fear of Black sexualities, while Henry Louis Gates Jr. (2013) wrote an equally intriguing essay for the *Root* describing the moment when sex was first engaged in Black literature. Still, Zora Neale Hurston is a controversial African American writer who paid the price for difference.

Hurston gained both admiration and notoriety during the Harlem Renaissance, and *Their Eyes Were Watching God* generated, and still generates, the most approbation and disapproval. Perhaps her harshest critic was male contemporary Richard Wright. Gates suggests that the root cause of Wright's displeasure with the work was "Hurston's creation of a black female protagonist who was comfortable with and celebrated her own sexuality, and who insisted on her right to choose her own lovers in spite of the strictures of the black community." In essence, Wright immediately gave *Their Eyes Were Watching God* a thumbs-down because Janie's profile did not align with the politics of respectability, because it did not present a Black woman who was happily married to a Black man who helped to uplift the race; Janie was supposed to have no significant role in her own uplift or the uplift of others, and she was definitely not supposed to imply that Black women (or men for that matter) were more or equally interested in sexual pleasure during this magnificent era of renaissance or Black rebirth. This type of protagonist and narrative, according to Wright's view, was not political enough to aid in the social advancement of the race. But does the race really advance if the baton carriers and torch-bearers are not self-identified, self-sexualized, and self-actualized? According to adrienne maree brown's definition, Hurston might very well be considered the African American community's first pleasure activist, one who allowed her wild pleasures to take her and her community to another level.[1]

The depictions of sexuality in *Their Eyes Were Watching God* are obviously not as explicit as those in some works today, but Hurston clearly did not take heed to cautions from Black presses suggesting that Black women keep their work free of depictions of overt sexuality. Her brief explanation of *Their Eyes Were Watching God* to librarian William Stanley Hoole demonstrates her precise disregard to the presses' attempts at policing respectability. Hurston avows:

> My next book is to be a novel about a woman who was from childhood hungry for life and the earth, but because she had beautiful hair, was always being skotched upon a flag-pole by

men who loved her and forced to sit there. At forty she got
her chance at mud. Mud, lush, and fecund with a buck Negro
called Teacake. He took her down into the Everglades where
people worked and sweated and loved and died violently,
where no such thing as flag-poles for women existed . . .
[T]his is the barest statement of the story. (*Zora Neale Hurston:
A Life in Letters* 366–67)

Indeed, this *is* the barest statement of the story, almost as bare as the
bodies of Tea Cake and Janie when they do the sweating and loving
that they do continuously and unapologetically throughout the text.
In addition to the "violent" manner in which Hurston's characters
practice everyday living in the Everglades, Hurston's 1937 terminology,
"mud, lush, and fecund," likewise, can easily be translated contemporarily to musk, lust, and fucking, as she both acknowledges and
rejects the flagpole that Black women were unwittingly "skotched" on.
Just as Bree Newsome, in a fit of rage, climbed up a thirty-foot pole
to remove the Confederate flag from that South Carolina statehouse
lawn, Hurston took a risky climb, nearly eight decades prior, to remove
the damaging instrument known as respectability politics. In doing
so, she attempted to grant freedom, not only to Janie, but to herself
and to all Black women who would follow.

Carla Kaplan (1995) insists that *Their Eyes Were Watching God* is
the story of a young woman in search of an orgasm; certainly, careful
readers can discern that her search was not in vain. For example, after
Janie has briefly gotten to know Tea Cake and fallen in love (or lust)
with him, the narrator portrays the following scene: "But she stayed
in bed long after he was gone. So much had been breathed out by the
pores that Tea Cake still was there. She could feel him and almost
see him bucking around in the upper air" (131–32). This premarital,
postcoital scene gives a brief depiction of the steam emanated between Janie and the "buck Negro" who, with his "bucking" (specifically
fucking, or engaging in aggressive, but pleasing, intercourse), makes
Janie's house feel less empty and "full uh thoughts, 'specially dat bedroom" (235). This point is especially important to note because while
Janie is the archetypal feminist character, a known staple in American
literature, no known critics deliberate over the fact that Janie does

indeed have premarital sex with Tea Cake. Despite lack of discussion, or perhaps in light of it, this passage supports the claim that one does not have to be a perfect character in order to serve as an inspiration to others. Still, many critics, namely Wright, could not look beyond Janie's body and bedroom to see her thoughts, could not fathom how the novel depicting the first orgasm in African American literature could likewise promote any positivity.

In the infamous pear tree scene, Hurston depicts sex (and orgasms) as an act as natural and beautiful as a blooming flower, stating:

> She was stretched on her back beneath the pear tree soaking in the alto chant of the visiting bees, the gold of the sun and the panting breath of the breeze when the inaudible voice of it all came to her. She saw a dust-bearing bee sink into the sanctum of a bloom; the thousand sister-calyxes arch to meet the love embrace and the ecstatic shiver of the tree from root to tiniest branch creaming in every blossom and frothing with delight . . . She had been summoned to behold a revelation. Then Janie felt a pain remorseless sweet that left her limp and languid. (307)

The fact that Janie is still a teenager when she first experiences the sensation of an orgasm—or is "summoned to behold a revelation"—foreshadows the overall development of her character. Janie, as Hurston suggests, "was from childhood hungry for life and the earth." Rebecca Walker, in her essay entitled "Lusting for Freedom" (2001), recognizes this hunger that young girls have and suggests that attention be paid to making sure that young women are capable of making "sex a dynamic, affirming, safe and pleasurable part of [their] lives" (22). In other words, Walker understands the importance of young women being nurtured among the fold of other self-identified, self-sexualized, and self-actualized women. She acknowledges the importance of not trying to convince girls that sexuality, sex, and pleasure are insignificant, invalidating, harmful, and disagreeable. As Janie learns, these phenomena are natural and can and should be powerful and exonerating.

When readers first encounter Janie in the opening lines of the novel, she is walking back into town after "burying the dead" and is

judged by the community of Eatonville (1). Her friend Pheoby leaves
the chatter and judgment of the porch and welcomes Janie home
by saying, "Gal, you sho looks *good*. You looks like youse yo' own
daughter" (5; emphasis original). Clearly, Pheoby uses this simile to
emphasize Janie's youthful appearance since the onlookers think that
Janie is anything but *good*. Still, this comparison is noteworthy because although Janie is sexual and has participated in the act of "baby
making," she does not have a baby, and particularly not a daughter.[2]
Furthermore, she has no mother or father (that she is aware of) and
has long since become apathetic to her deceased grandmother. In essence, Janie is both a motherless child and a childless mother, according to Pheoby's philosophy, all of which play a major role in how she
develops as a woman and as a character. Her sexuality, though slightly
constrained by a rigid upbringing, is a great part of her identity and
an even greater part of her life choices. Rightly so, in the foreword to
a later edition of the novel, Edwidge Danticat grapples with Janie's life
choices and lack of mother(hood), along with critical opinion of her
character, and ultimately determines that "Janie did not have to be a
role model at all. She simply had to be a fully realized and complex
character . . ." (xv). This she is indeed.

Although Hurston gives a brief glimpse of Janie's life as a child,
readers come to really know Janie at the age of sixteen, as Janie, too,
comes to know herself, when "her conscious life . . . commence[s]
at Nanny's gate" (13). At this moment of consciousness, Janie allows
Johnny Taylor to "lacerate" her with a kiss (15). The fact that Nanny
is half asleep during the escapade and awakens to establish that the
kiss is a laceration, or a deep wound, that Johnny must have violently
forced on Janie, early on distinguishes Janie's dreams and realities
from those of Nanny's and foreshadows their ever-evolving difference
of opinion on womanhood and sexuality. After the infamous pear
tree scene and continuously throughout the narrative, Janie's age and
sexuality combined are the center of unrest for both Janie and the
communities of individuals she encounters: from being sixteen and
married off to an older man who "don't even never mention nothin'
pretty," to finding out that she is no longer sexually attracted to her
second husband at "twenty-four and seven years married," to being
thirty-five and having her youth and womanhood mocked by Joe's

accusation that her "rump hang[s] nearly to [her] knees," and ultimately being forty and marrying the twenty-something Tea Cake
and coming back to town after his death in overalls as opposed to a
dress, "wid her hair swingin' down her back lack some young gal" (28,
85, 94, 2). These different experiences and obstacles contribute to the
complexity of Janie's character and support the claim that a character
with an active sexuality is more dynamic, round, sophisticated, and
ultimately more realistic. Furthermore, they serve as an outright dis-
avowal of respectability politics, a representation of the author's protest against rigid gender roles that yield little to no personal pleasure.

Along with Janie's age, her economic status has a deep impact
on her identity and the extent to which she practices her sexuality.
A common stereotype in African American literature and society is
that of the "jezebel, whore, or 'hoochie'" (*Black Feminist Thought* 81).
According to Patricia Hill Collins, jezebel "may be a 'pretty baby,' but
her actions as a 'hot mamma' indicate that she just can't get enough.
Because jezebel or the hoochie is constructed as a woman whose
sexual appetites are at best inappropriate and, at worst, insatiable, it
becomes a short step to imagine her as a 'freak'" (83). Also intrinsic
to jezebel's identity is the proclivity to use her body and sexuality for
financial gain. Overall, Collins suggests, "Because efforts to control
Black women's sexuality lie at the heart of Black women's oppression,
historical jezebels and contemporary 'hoochies' represent a deviant
Black female sexuality" (81). According to society's standard, via Collins, Hurston's Janie may be thought even more deviant than a jezebel.
Here's why: while Janie has an insatiable appetite for a "marriage,"
she does not see marriage in the usual way; it is physical and sensual.
Essentially, her idea of marriage is one teeming with encounters with
"visiting bees" that sink into the sanctum of her bloom and fulfill her
desire for perpetual orgasms. So, there is no surprise that Janie was
"married" three times. Even more, she is fiscally stable throughout
the narrative and is not personally seeking financial gain. Even as a
child living with Nanny, she is provided the best possible lifestyle for a
young Black girl being raised by a house servant and domestic worker.
She recognizes the power of socioeconomic stability but oftentimes
rejects materialistic offers along with the status these materials afford
her. In this sense, Janie defies the jezebel stereotype and cannot be

pigeonholed or categorized; she desires intimacy and pleasure over goods and status. She has the audacity to be wealthy and desirous of sex for no other reason but simple pleasure. Again, she sees it as a natural and free (read public) part of her life, and her acquaintances are neither prepared for nor appreciative of this oddity and demonstrate such in their criticism.

Upon Janie's return to Eatonville, the townspeople seem little concerned with her physical and mental well-being and more concerned with her physical appearance and material possessions. They ponder, "Where's dat blue satin dress she left here in?—Where all dat money her husband took and died and left her? . . . Where she left that young lad of a boy she went off wid? . . . Where he left *her*?—What he done wid all her money? . . . why she don't stay in her class?" (2). Ultimately, staying in her class would mean that the townspeople would have more access to Janie; to the community, it would mean that she would be more rooted and stable, less of a hot mamma. This, despite her financial situation, would make her easier to tolerate and control, less questionable, and therefore less powerful. Hurston implies that the natives of Eatonville, who seem to live according to outdated gender standards similar to Nanny's, are inwardly jealous of Janie, not simply because of her economic status, but because she lives an affluent life, is self-identified, and does not agonize over the politics of respectability, especially where sexuality is concerned. So, the members of the community, particularly the women, hope to use what they assume to be a decline in economic status as a weapon against her overall self-assurance and strength: "The women took the faded shirt and muddy overalls and laid them away for remembrance. It was a weapon against her strength . . ." (3). Because these women are governed by the politics of respectability, they erroneously assume that Janie's strength is a result of her class only, when it is due in large part to her unapologetic sexuality.

Janie's return to Eatonville is a precursor to Amber Rose's "Walk of No Shame," a 2015 comedic video in which the model/actress is seen in the early morning leaving an affluent home, wearing a tight-fitting black dress, and carrying her heels in her hand. She smiles proudly as she meets the milkman, an older woman walking a dog, a couple playing chess, working men, a family at the park, and a paperboy. They utter refrains such as the following: "It looks to me like you had sex last night," "It seems as though that woman hasn't been home since last night," "You're an inspiration to my daughter," and "I respect that you enjoyed yourself last night." Unlike Janie's counterparts, in this ideal world imagined by Amber Rose, society understands, respects, and appreciates when women express their sexualities unapologetically. At the end of the video, the mayor of this fictitious city even awards Rose the key to the city as a result of "[her] confidence, and the choices [she makes], and the ability to celebrate [her] body." On the contrary, Janie is not awarded a key to Eatonville, and respectability politics have not magically disappeared. As one of the wealthiest women in the town, though, she essentially already has the key. She also has the courage and strength to reject/ignore respectability politics, and these are the characteristics the residents of Eatonville envy the most.

By and large, courage and strength are what both separate Janie from and make her closer to the members of her communities. In order to be able to die peacefully, one of Nanny's main concerns is that Janie does not allow "de menfolks white or black [to make] a spit cup outa" her (24). In essence, she wants Janie to refrain from being the "mule uh de world" and avoid being used and controlled by, as well as forced to carry the burdens of, a patriarchal society (18). Ironically, Nanny assumes that the way to alleviate and reduce Janie's chances of becoming a mule is to marry her off to a man who specializes in and has gained his wealth by handling mules. When Janie is unsatisfied with her first marriage, Nanny consoles her by saying, "Youse uh married 'oman. You got yo' lawful husband same as Mis' Washburn or anybody else! . . . You come heah wid yo' mouf full uh foolishness . . . Heah you got uh prop tuh lean on all yo' bawn days, and big protection, and everybody got tuh tip dey hat tuh you and call you Mis' Killocks" (27). Oddly enough, during Janie's short marriage to Logan, Joe Starks is the only person to tip his hat to Janie and acknowledge her as Mrs. Killocks, only days before he runs away with her and provides a lifestyle for her that moves the community of Eatonville to tip their hats off to her and call her Mrs. Starks. Nanny could not fathom, as many proponents of respectability fail to address, why marriage does not equate to happiness, at least not marriage in its legal sense. Janie's idea of marriage was purer, as it required a physical and spiritual connection, two bodies and two souls joined together as one.

Still, even after Joe's death, residents of Eatonville "were all so respectful and stiff with her, that she might have been the Empress of Japan. They felt it was not fitting to mention desire to the widow of Joseph Starks" (112). Despite what would be Nanny's presumed posthumous appreciation for and satisfaction with this royal treatment, Janie is more concerned with the fulfillment of desires, which is why despite the community's disapproval, "she goes sashaying off to a picnic in pink linen [with Tea Cake and] . . . Done took to high heel slippers and a ten dollar hat" (135), having what Megan Thee Stallion calls a "hot girl summer." Disapproval aside, however, "They had to give it to her, she sho looked good, but she had no business to do it. It was hard to love a woman that always made you feel so wishful" (143). This purported lack of right is a result of oppressive cultural norms, those which Janie disregards. She states, "Dis ain't no business proposition, and no race after property and titles. Dis is uh love game. Ah done lived Grandma's way, now Ah means tuh live mine" (139). According to Cardi B.'s logic, Janie refrains from being a good girl who does what she is told and becomes a bad girl who does what she wants, but although Janie rejects Nanny's way, one could maintain that she fulfills Nanny's desire of not being the mule of the world and allowing men to use her. In fact, after Janie leaves the man that Nanny forces on her and realizes that Joe Starks, likewise, is not the man of her dreams, she goes out into the world and seemingly takes reign of the mule and fertilizes the earth with her own spit, and perhaps other white secretions as well.

Some may be concerned that while Janie did not become a mule, she may have become a Bitch, and if we reframe our thinking of the term, we might see that this is not necessarily a "bad" thing. Indeed, Janie is demanding, knows what she wants, and wanders from place to place until she finds what she is looking for. In essence, she "puts her looks, sexuality, intellect, and/or aggression to service," and, according to Patricia Hills Collins (and Cardi B.), that makes her a "Bad Bitch" (*Black Sexual Politics* 124). Collins notes that *Bitch* with the capital *B* has been contemporarily adopted as a term of endearment and power, as opposed to *bitch* with a lowercase *b*, which is an offensive term "designed to put women in their place" (123). Perhaps this is more clearly the reason for Wright's disdain with Hurston's work: during a time when traditional activists were beaten, maligned, and downtrodden by the fight for racial equality, Hurston managed to create a female character that rejected everyone's idea of her "place," prioritized her own personal pleasures, and still succeeded in enlightening and uplifting others. However, Janie's best friend, hoping to one day become a Bad Bitch herself, is the only person in Eatonville who openly appreciates Janie's ability to be a Bad Bitch and to share with others the knowledge she gained after going "tuh de horizon and back" (234). Pheoby proclaims, "Ah done growed ten feet higher from jus' listenin' tuh you, Janie. Ah ain't satisfied wid myself no mo'... Nobody better not criticize yuh in mah hearin'" (235). This viewpoint is significantly different from Pheoby's initial demand that Janie avoid being the topic of gossip by making "haste and tell 'em" all about her relations with Tea Cake and the financial situation he left her in (7). As a result of Janie's abilities to create her own path and act as a Bad Bitch, she has helped Pheoby to start on the path of becoming a self-identified individual and built a stronger camaraderie between the two friends. Such is the process of maverick feminism.

Furthermore, although only Pheoby admits her growth, each individual in the community, particularly the women, arguably benefit from Janie's experience. In her essay titled "Crayon Enlargements of Life: Zora Neale Hurston's *Their Eyes Were Watching God* as Autobiography" (1990), Nellie McKay insists, "Exchanging outsideness for individuality within the community, Janie becomes a feminist heroine with an assured place within that community, and her life becomes an influential source through which other women will find a model for their own self-empowerment" (68). Similarly, Barbara Christian, in *Black Women Novelists* (1980), notes the difference in Janie's perspective on her return versus the community's perspective, stating, "Janie does not see her life as tragic; she sees it as full and rich. It is essentially this message that she brings back to her community, that self-fulfillment rather than security and status is the gift of life" (59). In noting this grand message sharing, this community building, one must not lose sight of the fact that Janie left the community as a result of a desire to fulfill her own individual dreams, dreams of endless sexual expression similar to the life of bees and plants, and her return is only a result of her bee losing his stinger and ultimately his life, preventing her from continuing her expression in that particular place: "Tea Cake is gone. And dat's de only reason you see me back here—cause Ah ain't got nothing to make me happy no more where Ah was at" (8). Thus, in relation to community, specifically as it pertains to Janie's departure and return, sexuality both prevails over and provides for, demonstrating again how strong a role sexuality can play in a woman's life. Understanding and practicing her sexuality gives her the courage, audacity, and power to reject tradition, to live a fulfilling life, and those life experiences become lessons that the community can learn and gain hope from.

The narration of *Their Eyes Were Watching God* is another indicator of the impression Janie had on her community as a result of sharing her individual dreams. Several critics past, namely Robert Stepto (1979) and Mary Helen Washington (1987), have found fault in the fact that Hurston does not allow Janie to tell her story completely in first person, insisting that the third-person narration takes away Janie's voice and makes her less powerful and therefore less of the heroine that feminist critics have praised. Stepto argues that the third-person narration implies that "Janie has not really won her voice and self after all," and Washington argues that the novel "represents women's exclusion from power, particularly from the power of oral speech" (166; 27). However, Deborah Clarke comes to Hurston's rescue in her 2001 essay titled "The Porch Couldn't Talk for Looking: Voice and Vision in *Their Eyes Were Watching God*," suggesting that "Janie's achievement of voice is critical to her journey of self-awareness, but the highly ambivalent presentation of voice in the novel indicates that voice alone is not enough . . . For Hurston, then, the construction of African American identity requires a voice that can make you see" (599–600). She goes on to suggest that Hurston's "privileging of 'mind pictures' over words . . . [indicates an] ability to use voice visually . . . [It also] provides a literary space for African American women to relate their experiences . . . [and ultimately] opens up different ways of conceptualizing the African American experience" (600). Clarke's mind pictures and visual voice theory acknowledge that Janie lives her identity out loud, that it can be seen and felt even if her first-person voice isn't heard. So, whereas other critics have seen Hurston's third-person narration as a flaw, Clarke sees it as a break from dominant tradition, one worthy of recognition and praise.

Still, each of these interpretations misses Hurston's personal argument for why the story is told partially in third person: "You can tell 'em what Ah say if you wants to. Dat's jus de same as me 'cause mah tongue is in mah friend's mouf" (7). Despite Janie's seeming lack of interest in sharing her story with the community, the above statement that she makes to Pheoby is a clear indication that she is willing to share, but because she has maverick feminist characteristics, she is simply not willing to sit in their presence and be mentally or physically burdened by the judgment of their one-dimensional, outdated thoughts and beliefs (7). Yet, she does as Joan Morgan insists and "giv[es] the gift of survival experiences freely," as she is not obligated to tell Pheoby her story in order for Pheoby to tell others (232). In essence, she participates in the oral tradition in which a message is conveyed through speech or song and passed down from one generation to the next. To say that this tradition has been praised by critics for the tremendous effect it has had on African American literature is an understatment, and to demean this same tradition in Hurston's *Their Eyes Were Watching God* is to suggest that the folktales and songs passed down for over nine generations have long since lost their influence and strength since they are not conveyed in first person.

As Clarke maintains, indeed, Janie's presentation of voice is not enough to indicate the extent to which her voice is powerful, which is why Hurston allows another narrator, or perhaps several narrators, to convey Janie's message, to make certain that even after Janie follows Tea Cake in death and is "finished feeling and thinking," her strength can still be known because her story can still be told, and her voice, therefore, can still be heard. One can assume that when Janie herself is not the narrator, it is someone who has gotten the message via her friend's mouth and (generations of) porch talk. Even further, one could argue that Janie is not at all telling her story, but rather people generations removed from the initial telling are relaying the tale and are incessantly reviving her voice by acting out the visual picture Clarke indicates. Ultimately, perpetuality is the most powerful standing one individual voice can attain, and Hurston grants

Janie this perpetuality. Janie's tongue-sharing friend declares to her neigbors, "If she got anything to tell yuh, you'll hear it" (5). She does not say that they will hear it from Janie, or when they will hear it, but it will, ultimately, still be Janie doing the telling because she relayed the initial story.

Overall, this argument indicates that Janie is a complex character whose sexuality plays a significant role in all aspects of her life—ranging from the age in which she matures to how she views her economic standing, how others interact with her, and, finally, the extent to which she is vocal. All in all, Janie's characteristics are representative of maverick feminist characteristics. However, while she has accomplished her goals and followed her own dreams, the ending of the narrative does suggest that Janie finds herself at a standstill.

After completing her tale, urging Pheoby to grow, and proclaiming that she has been to the horizon and back, Janie mounts the stairs of her house as "everything around downstairs was shut and fastened" (236). This line does not simply pertain to the physical infrastructure of the house; everything is shut off in the downstairs area of Janie's body as well. One can assume that this is due in part to Hurston's cognizance that, ultimately, society sees free and open sexuality as a reason for punishment. In other words, Hurston is aware that she can lead readers (particularly African American women during this time) to the waters of self-identification, self-sexualization, and self-actualization, but she cannot make them drink. While she makes a conscious effort to take her heroine down from the flagpole, she realizes that society will see her radicalness as indictable, and she therefore punishes Janie accordingly.

Rebecca Walker insists, "For giving our bodies what they want and crave, for exploring ourselves and others, we are punished like Eve reaching for knowledge" (23). In Janie's case, her Eve-like punishment is the loss of her Adam, and therefore the ending to her real-life dream. So, while Janie gets freed of charges for Tea Cake's death and escapes the physical infrastructure of the prison, she pays for her other "crimes" with a punishment more serious than a jail sentence and is forced to return to Eatonville lacking the object of her quest: a marriage, a bee for her bloom.[3] This is not to say that Janie is not self-actualized or that her journey is without good cause. Rather, although

Hurston broke many grounds by allowing a young, Black woman to possess proudly an active and overt sexuality in 1937, she was a realist, aware that even the most progressive critics of her day could not fathom the thought of a Black, female character living happily and sexually ever after. Hence, Janie's hot girl summer abruptly came to an end.

GIRLS NEED LOVE: WINTER'S FIGHT FOR SURVIVAL

As a conscious rapper, writer, and activist, Sister Souljah has dreams of "improving cultural, economic, and social conditions" (*The Coldest Winter Ever* 459). Her politics are aligned with Black Nationalism as opposed to Black feminism, but the tale of Winter Santiaga in *The Coldest Winter Ever* is undoubtedly akin to a feminist tale. In fact, Janie's search in *Their Eyes Were Watching God* paves the way for sojourners such as Winter.

The Coldest Winter Ever is thought to be the revitalization of the urban novel after works such as Robert Beck's (also known as Iceberg Slim) *Pimp* (1969) and Donald Goines's *Dopefiend* (1971) had gone out of vogue. Winter's character is highly influenced by the drug culture that these two male writers provide vivid insight into, but Souljah divorces her work from theirs, insisting that although many had told the story of the rise of the drug kingpin, few had focused on the "fall of a drug kingpin, and how he descends back into poverty and slavery" (437). She admits to being more concerned with the effects this rise and fall have on those the kingpin was supposed to protect and provide for, how the "world pimps his unprotected daughters and dwarfs then devours his sons." In other words, it is not the kingpin's violence and ill-gained riches that Souljah wants to highlight. On the contrary, she urges that it is the violence that the world inflicts on his unsuspecting and unprotected offspring that garners immediate attention. Souljah insists, "I wanted to suck the romanticism out of those blockbuster books and films . . . to allow female characters to speak free from cultural domination or projections of how others thought we are" (437–38). And so enters Winter Santiaga, a young Black girl with little guidance, a spicy attitude, and a heightened sexuality.

With these characteristics, she is both America's nightmare and its sacrificial lamb.

Sister Souljah includes herself as a character in the novel—not as a maverick feminist because her politics are more centered on race than gender, but as a positive female influence and sociopolitical activist nonetheless—but Winter fervently rejects her guidance, insisting that "she's always talking some African mumbo jumbo" (46). And because Winter recognizes the problem with imitation and following a model—the fact that it allows little room for deviation and individuality—she finds herself on a lonely journey for self-identity and self-fulfillment, a journey that, like Janie's, is thrilling and adventurous as well as desolate and sad. Because of her experiences, her life and narrative—bad attitude, sexual recklessness, and all—serve as a cautionary tale from which other young Black women can learn, grow, and become empowered. Both she and Janie are presented as independent thinkers who reject respectability politics and "shake up the backward notions of womanhood" (Souljah 469). Ultimately, their authors recognized that the protagonists' independence was tantamount to the growth and progression of the women in their immediate communities as well as Black communities as a whole.

Told in a more traditional manner than Hurston's novel, *The Coldest Winter Ever*, narrated solely by Winter, begins with her literal birth, and ends, like *Their Eyes Were Watching God*, with the protagonist's sexual death and imprisonment. The opening lines depict Winter's birthday, or the moment she "came busting out of [her] momma's big coochie on January 28, 1977, during one of New York's worst snowstorms" (1); the closing lines of the novel paint an opposite view of both Winter and the city, however. She states, "When we got to the city, I was placed in a prison vehicle. New York street sounds brought back memories of so many things. Mostly memories of freedom. Being able to go to the store or the movies. Getting fucked in a parked car by the river or in the grass or on the back of stairs . . . I'm doing fifteen years for having a bad attitude" (425).

Winter's recollection of the city is not much unlike the one Janelle Monáe envisions in her Afrofuturistic emotion picture, *Dirty Computer* (2018), where she rejects and critiques government, marriage, religion, and heteronormativity and even fancies getting *screwed* "on a holiday . . . at a matinee . . . at a festival . . . like an animal." Like Winter, Monáe is captured and imprisoned for not following the rules of what she calls a totalitarian society. Social workers and friends all try to convince Winter to stay in a group home and abide by the system's rules after she is unexpectedly separated from her parents and a cushiony lifestyle at the age of sixteen—the same age as Janie's awakening—but she is adamant about being independent and taking care of herself by her own means. The end result is serving time in the prison building that Hurston seemingly allowed Janie to escape, an imprisonment that society has deemed necessary for those, especially young Black women, who do not adhere to sexual norms, have "bad attitudes," and do not uphold other facets of respectability politics.

In "Lusting for Freedom," Rebecca Walker reveals to readers the age of her first sexual encounter, stating, "If you are a girl, sex marks you, and I was marked at a young age. I am too ashamed to tell people how young I was, but I am too proud to lie. Eleven. I was eleven" (20). She discloses this very personal information in hopes of shifting traditional attitudes and conversations (or the lack thereof) regarding respectability and sexuality. In other words, if this experience is essentially inevitable, then preparation and conversation should be inevitable as well.

Winter is indeed marked at a young age, and she has several conversations with her parents and peers about sex and sexuality, but none of them are constructive or logical. In fact, her immediate circle has conflicting views. Winter's mother is convinced that "when a woman wants to get fucked, she gets fucked. She gets fucked whether it's in a car or a closet," so she gets Winter a prescription for birth control pills and sends her out into the world to get fucked, literally and figuratively (8). On the other hand, Winter is a daddy's girl; her father is certain that she is "not a woman yet" and cautions her that "only a hardworking man, a sharp thinker who doesn't hesitate to do what he gotta do, to get you what you need to have, deserves you" (9). The problem is that she has blurred visions of what she needs to have, so the sharp thinkers on the corners who watched, amazed, as her "titties sprouted" in just "one year, from age twelve to thirteen" excite her (8). This excitement brings about curiosity, curiosity that is cured in an apartment when no parents or adults are around to object or cause further confusion. Winter states, "Chanté, who was older than us, taught us all the sexual positions. She let us watch while she got down with boys when her mother was at work. She liked the idea of being our 'teacher.' She even taught us how to suck a dick" (17). One can only imagine how a dick-sucking lesson is carried out, especially when a living, breathing human serves as the prop. The author does not leave readers wondering how her protagonist uses these lessons, though, as several sex scenes depict Winter practicing and exercising her misguided discipline. Neither Chanté nor Mrs. Santiaga is self-identified, self-sexualized, or self-actualized; instead, their lifestyles, choices, and actions are dependent on others. Therefore, they are not the best "teachers" for Winter; unfortunately, she only comprehends their inadequacies once she is alone and has experienced trauma due to lack of logical and practical preparation.

Winter's description of her first sexual encounter is a prime example of teachings gone wrong. She and her friends got their "cherries busted" and "lied to each other about how good the first time felt." In hindsight, however, she acknowledges the following: "The truth was those big dicks ripped our tight little twelve-year-old tunnels apart" (16). Even with her father out of prison, Winter had little guidance and protection; thus, one can only imagine the age of "those big dicks." Were the girls technically raped? At twelve, surely, they were not at the age of consent. Unfortunately for Winter, her problems are only just beginning. There is more pimping for the world to do.

Several years after this occurrence, Winter has another violent sexual encounter that is exemplary of the ill-advised and convoluted teachings of her past. This experience takes place when she is eighteen, has undergone an abortion, and is afraid to tell her controlling, drug-dealing boyfriend. The long, but pertinent scene is the most vivid and most telling for both Winter and her readers:

A dick-suck cures everything. So I unfastened Bullet's belt, dropped down to my knees and went to work. I centered myself so he could see my lips sucking and pulling. So he could see my tongue. He needed to know he was the boss. I had no problem with that. When I saw his mouth open wide, a look of pain covered his face, but I knew it was just the ecstasy of him busting in my mouth . . . He rolled on his side with another hard on. He began to undo my pants. "I'm on my period," I said, trying not to panic. I bent over to lick his balls again. He pulled my head up and said, "A nigga wants pussy. This is my pussy, right?" he questioned. I answered with a nod. "A little blood ain't gonna hurt this big dick." He was all up in me. How can I describe this feeling? It wasn't pleasure. It wasn't pain. It was nothing, like a dick plunging into an ocean. But still I conjured up some moans for him. (406–7)

All of the advice Winter received from her father, mother, and Chanté proves to be ineffective in this scene: Bullet has proven that he is willing to work hard to give her what she thinks she needs (mainly material goods), but he is anything but the gentleman her father had hoped she would attract and desire. Furthermore, Winter's "titties" that magically grew are not appealing to Bullet as he is more interested in "his pussy." And the long nights spent with Chanté in her dick-sucking class do not pay off. But most importantly, Winter learns that the world can be cruel, and sometimes women "get fucked" even when they don't want to. Again, she is raped but does not recognize it as such, or rather thinks that getting fucked is her only option. She has a heightened sexuality, but she is not yet self-sexualized; there is a difference. Through this experience and others, she learns that sex and sexuality, although powerful, are not and should not be the sum of her existence. Furthermore, there should be pleasure for both parties when sex is practiced in a healthy and holistic manner.

The abovementioned scene is different from that of Janie and Tea Cake's when they, too, have a very physical sexual interaction. As Tea Cake and Janie are disputing Tea Cake's presumed infidelities with Nunkie, a "little chunky girl" on the muck, Hurston's narrator insists, "They wrestled on until they were doped with their own fumes and emanations; till their clothes had been torn away; till he hurled her to the floor and held her there melting her resistance with the heat of his body, doing things with their bodies to express the inexpressible; kissed her until she arched her body to meet him and they fell asleep in sweet exhaustion" (169). This scene, literally, is hot and steamy. Although it begins as a dispute concerning a potential mistress, it quickly turns into reciprocated lovemaking, as the two have a mutual passion and maturity where sexuality is involved. This is the woman Hurston wanted to take down from the flagpole. This is the mud, lush, and fecund that she wrote to William Stanley Hoole about. Janie's relationship with Tea Cake and her adventures away from the town of respectability—that is, Eatonville—have taught her that, although physical, sex is a mental and emotional union that should be pleasurable and fulfilling to both partners. "The next morning," Hurston suggests, "Janie asked like a woman" if Tea Cake was in fact involved with Nunkie, instead of repeating previous actions of drawing ill-advised conclusions and inflicting violence on her mate.

In terms of asking and acting "like a woman," linguist Denise Troutman (1995) suggests, "One mark of attaining womanhood is knowing when to be polite and when to assert oneself" (214). Winter and her mother seem to be learning this lesson simultaneously. For instance, when Winter's father tells the family about the unexpected move from Brooklyn to Long Island only months before his incarceration, Winter proclaims, "I did something that I normally wouldn't do. I questioned Santiaga" (15). In a similar manner, although Winter does not verbally question her mother while her mother and father are having a disagreement, she mentally questions her and determines the importance of voice while realizing when and how she must utilize hers. Winter insists, "The tone of mother's voice was rare. I can hardly say I ever remember it being this rough . . . I expected Santiaga to yell back but he didn't. Instead mother just continued blowing her cool and doing something she told me not to do" (44). It is in this moment, one can conclude, that Winter determines that even if "role models" existed, her mother is not the best model to follow, especially since her mother does not follow her own advice.

Essentially, the veil has been lifted from Winter's eyes. It is not until the end of the novel, though, that she begins to fully grasp an understanding of the power and advantages (or disadvantages) of sexuality. Likewise, because her parents have provided her with so many distorted images, economics is also a subject that she has to relearn after her father is imprisoned, as money is also a driving force in her identity and actions. In the same breath as the pulsating description of her birth, Winter assures readers, "Brooklyn-born I don't have no sob stories for you about rats and roaches and pissy-pew hallways" (1). Though vulgar, this statement is also unapologetic and suggests to readers that despite the events that follow—some indeed tragic and deplorable—sympathy or pity is unnecessary, as the twenty-five-year-old narrator, after reflecting on her life experiences, is headed in the direction of becoming a self-identified woman. In retrospect, she boldly embodies the message of her author, signifying that there is no one way to be a Black woman. Really, this new understanding is inevitable after the lifestyle she had known is no more; she is left to fend for herself and unlearn all of the falsehoods presented by her mother and father.

According to Winter's mother, the "finer" the woman, the finer things she should expect to receive because beauty "was a full-time occupation that left no room for anything else . . . [and] beautiful women are supposed to be taken care of" (4). By taken care of, she means provided with name-brand clothes, shoes, jewels, and a lavish home worth bragging about. Winter states, "One thing I learned from my mother is a bad bitch gets what she wants if she works her shit right" (11). Souljah implies that, unfortunately, neither Winter nor her mother knew exactly what "her shit" was. They did not own or possess anything, not even themselves. In a similar manner, her father, Santiaga, suggests, "You, Winter, you deserve better. You deserve to relax, kick back, have the easy and finer things in life. No stress. One of these big-headed doctors, lawyers, engineer boys around this neighborhood can give you that. A man in Midnight's line of work can't" (69). Interestingly enough, Santiaga seems to want to raise a *respectable* and modest daughter despite the fact that he married a woman who is vain, vulgar, and rambunctious. His notions are reminiscent of Nanny's insistence that Janie marry a wealthy landowner with an organ in his parlor, have a prop to lean on, and have people tip their hats off to her as a sign of respect. Of course, there is no crime in a father wanting a better life for his daughter. Still, Midnight is Winter's dream, her idea of a husband. Even more, the tall, chocolate, toned, young man is Santiaga's immediate assistant, which means that they are both in the same "line of work." If Midnight cannot provide Winter with what she needs from a mate, can her father provide what she needs from a parent? This is the ultimate question that Souljah raises with this text.

Unsurprisingly, the answer is no, Santiaga does not provide Winter with what she needs, not while he is free to roam the streets and conduct his illegal business, and definitely not while he is imprisoned. Because their entire way of life has depended on sex and money, although neither of the two entities are bad when practiced and used adeptly, their whole family structure falls apart when the men are imprisoned. In the beginning of the novel, community seems to be very important to Winter as she boasts about how close she and her family and friends are. She acknowledges her familial bond, stating, "I had three aunts, four uncles, and a whole slew of cousins. As far as we were concerned, it was live for all of us to be chilling in the same building, or at least the next building over. We never had to worry about getting into fights because around our way, we had a reputation . . . Everybody understood that our family had the neighborhood locked down" (2). Similarly, she discusses how she and her girlfriends "were mad tight, many of us born and raised in the same spot . . . we did everything together" (16). This closeness and respect only existed when her family's wealth existed, however, because when the money stopped piling in, the people started filing out. Of course, Winter plays a role in how people treat her, as she goes about life selfishly, not truly thinking about the feelings of others. Nonetheless, she realizes that there is a distinct difference in the way that people, specifically men, treat her after "Santiaga got knocked" (225). Winter's family members' and friends' identities and actions are dependent on someone else, and the absence of that someone else presents room for uncharacteristic behaviors. Whereas Winter's mother turns to drugs, her family members turn to thievery. None were self-identified, self-sexualized, or self-actualized, and they offered little assistance in nourishing these same characteristics in others. As a result, the progress that Winter makes toward the end of the novel is entirely due to her isolation from and reflections on the trauma experienced at the hands of those who were supposed to protect her.

For instance, after living in various places, Winter returns to her Brooklyn neighborhood and resides with her Aunt B. Aunt B expects payment for her generosity. Winter notes, "I woke up that afternoon to Aunt B wanting a loan. Since I wasn't crazy, and Aunt B's husband was locked up with my father, I knew that if I gave her any money, I'd never get it back" (158). Unbeknownst to Winter, she would also never get back loyalty, as Aunt B steals money from Winter's underwear while she is showering and releases her to child welfare. After this incident, Winter insists, "I decided I would think of everyone in my family as dead" (206).

In a similar manner, while Winter may have initially implied that she and her friends did everything together, some things she decides that they do not do well together are date the same man and wear the same quality of clothes. Winter learns that her supposed best friend is dating a notable, up-and-coming drug dealer and wearing the fashions that only she had once been known for. While at a concert, she insists, "Everything was cool until I saw [Natalie] standing up, clapping with a sky blue thirty-five-hundred-dollar Chanel skirt-suit on. This bitch pops out of nowhere with some wears that was strictly my style and over-reaching for her . . . My body shook with anger at Santiaga and Mom . . . Now what was I supposed to do while Natalie was up there pretending to be me?" (162–63). Winter acknowledges that she is mostly in this predicament because her parents failed her, and Natalie uses their noted failure to her advantage, insisting that Winter is not on her level because she has a "crazy-ass crackhead, bald-headed mother," and Winter herself is "*broke* [and] homeless" (168; emphasis original). It is clear that Winter's mother and father had failed her long before they were, respectively, addicted to drugs and imprisoned. They failed her because they did not teach her the importance of being self-identified, self-sexualized, and self-actualized. Vain ideals such as beauty and materialism and outdated beliefs such as respectability were the extent of their teachings and desires. Janie's character, decades before Winter, exemplified the notion that these characteristics and practices added together do not equal a whole, independent, fulfilled, or revolutionary individual.

Therefore, and to no surprise, it is after these experiences and during moments of isolation that Winter's character becomes more complex. She begins to discover that while sex and sexuality are beautiful and powerful entities, they cannot be the sum of one's existence. Even more, this text suggests that, especially when attempting to navigate the world alone, a Black woman will experience more positive results when she is self-identified, self-sexualized, and self-actualized. As such, when Winter does not have her community and is forced to fend for herself, with the exception of recurring thoughts and dreams of Midnight, her sexuality and desires for sensual pleasures take a backseat to other forms of success and fulfilment that are not for plaudits of people but for sustainment of well-being and self-pleasure.

For example, when taken by child welfare to an all-girls group home called the House of Success, she uses her people skills and knowledge of fashion to become an entrepreneur and gain an extensive clientele. Winter states, "I spent every day up until Friday getting to know the girls in the house . . . Who had extra money and what kind of taste they had . . . My first customer, the person I volunteered to be my best customer, was Claudette. I figured if I could fix her up, make her pay for it, she'd be a good example of what my work was worth" (193–95). Interestingly, Winter makes enough money to support herself from her room while her loyal customers, the remaining girls in the home, go out on a daily basis to work for others. She proclaims, "At the end of twenty-one days, I had two thousand five hundred dollars in my pocket, and I had never left my room" (198). Undoubtedly, minor knowledge of her father's business helped Winter to understand the influence of supply and demand, a skill that helped her become successful in the House of Success, but imagine how much of a success she might have been had she had positive, self-identified, self-sexualized, and self-actualized influencers and allies helping her to more positively channel these skills. Ultimately, when young girls and women have strong and positive circles to begin with, they learn to use their sexualities and wits as a means to fulfill self as opposed to pimping themselves out for love and protection.

Because the narrative ends with Winter incarcerated, one can conclude that her story is presented as a cautionary tale. Nevertheless, at one of the most pivotal points in the narrative, when she can impart wisdom to her younger sister, Porsche, she chooses to remain silent. Seeing her teenage sister for the first time in over seven years at their mother's funeral and assuming that Porsche—dressed provocatively and "pushing a whip it would take the U.S. president's salary to pay for"—is following a similar path as her, Winter states, "I wanted to warn her about certain things in life. Usually I'm not at a loss for words. But I didn't feel good enough to tell her what I really thought.

I knew she would think: Winter, you're just saying that 'cause you're in jail . . . old . . . ugly . . . jealous. Instead of saying what I had learned, what was on the tip of my tongue, I said nothing at all . . . She'll learn for herself. That's just the way it is" (428, 430). This final statement emphasizes the sheer hypocrisy of doing things merely for tradition's sake—that is, the way they were always done—especially when tradition has not proven to be rewarding.

Indeed, Winter learned her lessons on her own, but she also experienced unnecessary trauma as a result. Now, despite possessing maverick feminist traits—being self-identified—and being completely aware that self-fulfillment is essential to the potential uplift of others, she misses her chance at true sisterhood for fear of sounding too preachy because she is not yet self-actualized. The African American community, particularly Black women in or beholden to the Woman's Convention, have shoved respectability politics down one another's throats for so long that, now, any sign of communal knowledge sharing is met with much hesitance and uncertainty. I argue, however, and *The Coldest Winter Ever* supports, that intentional sisterhoods and intergenerational relationships can be beneficial for all involved when they are practiced effectively. Effective practice means acknowledging that the journey of lifting as we climb requires admitting that each individual has particular strengths as well as a voice and desires that should not be ignored. In other words, the mere fact that one is more experienced does not suggest that their life is a model or mandate that others are required to follow, as, ultimately, there is no one way to be a whole and thriving Black woman.

Unfortunately, as demonstrated in *Their Eyes Were Watching God* and again in *The Coldest Winter Ever*, because we live in a society where individuality and an unapologetic sexuality are feared and frowned on, the consequences individuals face for charting their own paths often come in the form of imprisonment or death, literal or sexual. This fact is particularly evident in *Life After Death* (2021), the sequel to *The Coldest Winter Ever*, as we find Winter speaking to readers for the majority of the book in a purgatory described as the "Last Stop Before the Drop." On her release date, and still up to her old ways even in her thirties, although now the star of her own reality show, Winter is shot by her "friend" Simone and in a coma. While in this coma, she experiences the hell of the Last Stop Before the Drop, and the only way she can overcome death is to be locked into a Truth Booth where she is confronted with her previous sexual adventures and must obtain mercy from, bow down to, and worship Allah. I have to admit that as a fan of Winter, I was not, initially, pleased with this second book. While I proclaim to be a Christian and believe in living a moral and just life, it is clear that this type of mercy is not all that Winter needs to become a new and whole being. More specifically, she is still not self-actualized and has made little to no progress in her personal/feminist journey because she does not reciprocate Porsche's sisterhood in this sequel. For example, the nurses explain to Winter that while she was in a coma, Porsche washed and combed her hair, gave her manicures and pedicures, massaged her legs, changed her body position, read stories to her, sang and talked to her, cried for her, and only left her side when it was absolutely necessary (328). Still, Winter admits that when it was time to be open and honest with her sister, she could not. She insists:

> That's how it was between me and my sister. I would always have something urgent that I wanted to say to her. But for some reason, I wouldn't. I knew the words to say. I knew clearly what I wanted her to know. Sometimes I wanted to tell her what I had learned from living life, also from getting shot dead, my afterlife, and my return to life. But then, my tongue would feel heavy. The words that needed to be spoken, I never spoke. Even before I was murdered, it was like that between me and my sister Porsche. My mind was reminding me of how I wanted to say certain things to her at my mother's funeral long ago. I had one opportunity and maybe even, only one minute to say some urgent things. I didn't. Even now I know I should thank her, tremendously. I know what she gave up to get us to this point. I know that she didn't have to do shit for me. She was already rich, married, chilling, a mother of three. She didn't have to bother at all. (330)

Though it is upsetting that Winter's only progress and redemption in *Life After Death* is religious and therefore seems to clasp her tighter in the grips of respectability politics, this passage is reassurance that she (and her author) realizes that there is more that needs to be done, that she is still in process, and that (positive) sisterhoods are important. For these reasons, even at the end of the sequel, Winter is still a cautionary tale; she is not a role model, but, indeed, girls and women can learn from her the importance of being self-identified, self-sexualized, and self-actualized.

SEXUALITY, CONFIDENCE, AND ADVOCACY: THE MEMOIR OF BRITTNEY COOPER

How much value and validity can we place on the narratives of fictional characters depicted in novels? In other words, do real-life, sexualized Black women suffer similar imprisonments in today's time as Janie and Winter did in previous years? The answer is yes! Too often we separate literature from life, not realizing or acknowledging the connections between authors' lived experiences and the literature they produce, how they both inform one another and impact the culture. Again, *Their Eyes Were Watching God*, *The Coldest Winter Ever*, and every other primary text discussed in this book are the respective author's intellectual contribution to affirming and improving the lived experiences of Black women and other marginalized communities in American society. *Eloquent Rage* by Brittney Cooper—professor and cultural critic—is no exception.

A recent study suggests that faculty of color are making an "endless exodus" from the academy in search of positions where they are fulfilled and can more directly impact marginalized communities. Journalist LaMont Jones insists that it simply takes too long to impact policy from the academy. This statement is not completely false, as the publication process itself is lengthy, and audiences are often limited to other scholars or students hoping to become scholars. However, this reality does not change the fact that the services of forward-thinking professors are necessary in preparing students for the world they currently live in as they await changes in policy to create the world they hope to live in. Policy changes begin with individual people, most times individual people who were students in the classrooms of progressive, advocating professors. Even more, many academics are now rising to the level of public figure and using the expertise acquired from and applied in the academy to impact broader ranges of audiences. Melissa Harris-Perry, Marc LaMont Hill, and Henry Louis Gates Jr. are but a few of these scholars-turned-celebrities who have worked tirelessly to bridge the gap between the academy and the streets.

Brittney Cooper, commended by Michael Eric Dyson as possibly "the boldest young feminist writing today," is increasingly climbing the ranks in both academia and popular culture and representing a diverse group of communities—Louisiana, the South, Black women, curvy girls, feminists, the Hip Hop generation, and Christians—each step of the way. Guest appearances on networks such as NPR, MSNBC, PBS, OWN, and BET are but a few of her enterprises into the public eye. The ability to expand her reach is due in part to the success of several books and periodicals, which are due in part to her academic training, but all, I argue, reflect her intentional relationships with women who are self-identified, self-sexualized, and self-actualized.

In her memoir, *Eloquent Rage: A Black Feminist Discovers Her Superpower*, Cooper depicts an upbringing and lifestyle different from those of the protagonists in Hurston's and Souljah's novels: she has yet to be married and therefore does not appear to have been pushed toward marriage or union in order to increase her socioeconomic standing or propensity to succeed. Good grades and (advanced) formal education, instead, seemed to be the expectation. However, she, too, lost her father at an early age and learned what it meant to fend and look out for herself as a latchkey child growing up in 1980s Louisiana. All in all, despite the positive divergences she seemed to have taken to avoid "becoming a statistic," Cooper, like Janie and Winter, determined that disregarding or depreciating one's sexuality is an unhealthy act. Likewise, espousing the politics of respectability, especially in this twenty-first century, is a suffocating and depressing endeavor. She insists, "We do a kind of violence to ourselves when we shut down our sexuality . . . Respectability tells us that staying alive matters more than protecting one's dignity. Black rage says that living without dignity is no life at all" (137, 165).

Cooper, now, supports the ideas of crunk feminism, of eloquent rage, of enjoying a "penis attached to a man who knows how to use it," but her narrative suggests that this radicalness, these maverick feminist characteristics, did not fully materialize until she was well into adulthood and became attached to a community of self-identified, self-sexualized, and self-actualized women (*Eloquent Rage* 22).[4] Before then, she admits that her existence was somewhat modest and narrow and that she was practicing the culture of dissemblance. Coined by Darlene Clark Hine (1989), the culture of dissemblance is a practice, or cult, of secrecy used by Black women as a coping mechanism in which they present themselves as asexual as a form of protection from society. In other words, out of some unknown fear, Cooper was not living a fulfilled, free, and unapologetic life. And although one does not have to be wild and promiscuous in order to be self-sexualized, it is clear that Cooper, in a sense, was in a self-inflicted prison. However, she shares her memoir in hopes that her experiences and intellectual thought will aid in the freedom and progression of other women, specifically Black women. Therefore, her work, like the narratives of Hurston and Souljah, serves as a form of advocacy and self-care, effectively bridging the gap between the academy and everyday life.

Self-care among Black women, particularly those who identify as feminists, Cooper learns, takes on a much-nuanced meaning. Essentially, however, because Black women, as Malcolm X noted, are the most disrespected, unprotected, and neglected group in America, self-care means prioritizing one's own preservation and pleasure. Throughout her memoir, Cooper acknowledges the fact that she did not often prioritize or accommodate herself. She recalls revealing to a "homegirl" that even as a woman in her thirties, orgasms were somewhat mystifying to her, as she could not figure out how to experience one that she herself did not cause, presumably through masturbation. Cooper notes, "She looked at me with a look of incredulity and thinly veiled disgust at the dudes I had slept with and said, 'Shit, I'll fuck you.'" Insisting that her homegirl was "only half-joking," Cooper determined that she seriously needed to "invest in [her] own pleasure" (22). In other words, she needed to practice what she preached; she needed to take herself down from the flagpole of respectability, a place where eroticism is thought to be a sinful weakness as opposed to a sensual power. More directly, she needed to be more like Hurston's Janie.

In hindsight, Cooper recognizes that as much as a decade before this particular "homegirl intervention" as she calls it, her grandmother had tried to be her muse, her wise counselor, her link in an intergenerational relationship, but, like Winter, she ignored the message. "It's time for you to start having sex," she recalls her Christian, seventy-five-year-old grandmother demanding. She insists that her twenty-two-year-old self was still "too much of a Christian zealot to be either pragmatic or feminist," stating:

> My grandmother didn't have all the language for these differing ideological positions, but she had good sense. She looked at me with those laser eyes that Black mamas use to see right through you, and commanded me to "start having sex." She meant real, good sex. Sex that left you with the telltale signs that you had been touched right and handled with care. I didn't exude sexuality. I didn't exude grown womanhood. I did not look like a Black girl comfortable in my own skin. Because I wasn't. (127)

Why was Cooper not comfortable in her own skin? Why was sex such a distressing topic? I am glad you asked, but this issue is much larger than any one individual.

With an unconscious and unyielding commitment to respectability and a religion that was forced on them by their oppressors, Black families have long been invested in negating the stereotypes of said oppressors and, therefore, often ignore or reject critical discussions on sex and sexuality, not realizing the connections one's sexuality has to everyday life and actions. Rebecca Walker discusses her change of character after having her first sexual encounter and becoming comfortable with and confident in her sexuality and insists that it translated into multiple aspects of her life. She maintains, "I was able to carry that pleasure and confidence into my everyday life working at the hair salon, raising my hand in English class, hanging out with my best girlfriend, and flirting with boys" (19). Cooper's grandmother seemed to have had a discerning spirit, but Cooper admits that she did not operate with this confidence, that until her thirties, while she was not a virgin, she had let respectability politics have the last word and had "traded being one kind of statistic for the other," thereby pleasing the spirits of early European settlers whom, I surmise, had no greater fear than confident, self-possessing, pleasure-seeking Black women (118).

While Cooper is clear that her grandmother and mother did not "preach" respectability politics to her just as Winter did not want to preach it to her sister, it is apparent that few around her preached against it. Knowing that her mother became pregnant at the age of eighteen, did not have the privilege of higher education, worked a tiresome and unfulfilling job, and often suffered at the hands of the men she loved, Cooper's manifesto was solidified early in her life: she took it upon herself to challenge stereotypes by keeping her legs closed and her books open—assuming that these practices would gain her the respect of others. As a maturing Black scholar, however, she soon learned that she rested on the wrong side of society's propensity to award unfair advantages and disadvantages and that, therefore, respect was not automatically given simply because one followed the rules. Instead, most times, she found that she was desexualized altogether, leaving her to question her own gaze. Ultimately, she determined that "though good behavior has its place, it's the disruptive girls, the loud, rowdy, attitudinal girls, and the defiant, quiet, insolent Black girls who expose every day exactly what this system is made of"—basically girls like those depicted in the novels of Hurston and Souljah (163). In essence, she rejects the covenant of the Woman's Convention which suggests that "good," content, rule-abiding Black people are the best advocates for the community. On the contrary, it is groundbreaking women with earth-shattering philosophies who reveal the most problems within society and resultantly affect the most change. To be clear, this theory does not encourage Black women all across the world to begin destroying their own communities under the guise of activism and change; conversely, maverick feminism requires an epistemological approach, a maturity that is gained first through self-evaluation and self-fulfillment.

This self-evaluation is akin to what Cooper calls being in process. For maverick feminists, the process is often initiated once in community with women who are also in process (like Winter) or women who have gone to the horizon and back (like Janie), women who exude a confidence and self-definition that one desires. Too often society shuns and dejects this confidence, especially among African American women, equating it to rebellion and defiance instead. But to paraphrase Toni Cade Bambara (1970), it is important to note that there is nothing rebellious or defiant about a Black woman who gets passionate about herself and her direction. In fact, this initially selfish act benefits entire communities because Black women have long since carried the notion that it is their duty to birth, protect, and uplift nations.

In example, after reflecting on education's impact on her life, Cooper insists, "I gained the tools to do better analytical work and ask better questions in the university. I became a feminist in a PhD program. Hell, I learned the word *epistemology* in a PhD program. But, more than all of that, I learned to heal from the anti-Black trauma and bullying that was the entirety of my childhood at *college*" (268). Though, in what seems to have become a post-self-reflection and post-healing requirement for Black women intellectuals (because activism), within a few breaths, she determines that she is now responsible and fit to fight for others, stating, "I'm not planning to go back home to live, because where I'm from is no place for a radical feminist Black girl who likes to challenge preachers in her spare time. But I am responsible in big and small ways for making that place and places like it better, more equitable and more just" (270). Although crediting her formal education for providing her with the tools to deal with the trauma of her personal life, Cooper acknowledges that there is indeed a difference between the walls of the academy and the alleyways of the streets. However, knowledge comes in many forms. And while the knowledge and resources she gained in the academy continue to offer a stage to fight for justice in her hometown and across the globe, the knowledge gained outside the classroom, while in conversation with her grandmother and homegirls, gave Cooper the courage and gall to fight for justice in her hometown and across the globe. In other words, maverick feminism, including sisterhoods and intergenerational relationships with women who are self-identified, self-sexualized, and self-actualized, was/is a saving grace and a provider, for Cooper as an individual and for her communities.

CONCLUSION

Zora Neale Hurston, with dexterity, paved the way for and impacted how contemporary Black women both read and write literature as well as how they live their everyday lives. Donna Williams (1994) describes a love-hate relationship that critics have had with Hurston because she did not attenuate her folk art with the political endeavors of the day, insisting, "If Zora Neale Hurston were walking the Earth today like a natural woman, folks would still, no doubt, be loving her or hating her with a vengeance. They'd either be inviting her to dinner, knowing that she would dominate the conversation . . . or they'd be running like crazy from her exasperating presence" (86). Because novels are often representatives of life, critics have equally mixed feelings about Hurston's most popular heroine, Janie Crawford.

Music enthusiasts suggest that Tupac Shakur foreshadowed his own death in numerous songs over the span of his rap career. Equally so, one could argue that Hurston foreshadowed the trajectory of her writing career through the story of Janie Crawford. Janie was accepted by and began her journey with the help of benefactors who wanted to limit and possess her. She was grateful, but she wanted more, so she set out on a very selfish and very fulfilling journey, had fun, gained knowledge, and shared knowledge, impacting the lives of more people than she could have ever imagined. When it was all said and done, however, she acknowledged that she resided in an orthodox world that did not appreciate her progressive prowess. So, she closed herself off and took the lonely climb to the top of the stairs, not to be seen again until decades later.

I am so grateful for Hurston's courage, and for her sass and ingenuity. And I am equally grateful for the likes of Alice Walker who realized that her life, and our lives, would be all the more fruitful with Hurston in it. Janie's story, as well as Winter's, is both unique and universal. The protagonists analyzed in this chapter are not model citizens and do not privatize their intimate feelings. Nevertheless, they are journeying figures who experience life and learn lessons that are beneficial to others. They experiment with sexuality, become self-identified, and ultimately deduce that womanhood is completely subjective. And while their narratives end with them bound in either a metaphorical or literal prison, they are metaphysically unrestrained, as they have relinquished the chains of respectability politics and encourage other women to do the same.

In sum, it is through the analysis of Hurston's own novel as well as Sister Souljah's *The Coldest Winter Ever* and Brittney Cooper's memoir, *Eloquent Rage*, that I have tried to affirm what Hurston discovered over four score ago: sex and sexuality play a significant role in the lives of Black women and therefore cannot be ignored. Moreover, self-identified, self-sexualized, and self-actualized women garner and exude an array of power and agency that influences and benefits others in their communities. Neither Christianity nor respectability politics can reduce or deter the impact. Cooper's narrative, specifically the progress and change she displays after having uncomfortable yet inevitable conversations with her grandmother and homegirls, brings to life Hurston's theory, presented by Pheoby, that one can grow "ten feet higher from jus' listenin'" to women who display maverick feminist–like characteristics. The act of sharing these stories is equivalent to imparting on others the necessary self-care tools that are often obtained in a sisterhood or intergenerational relationship. Ultimately, I argue that more of us should be like Hurston and put our "tongues in our friends' mouths." As I illustrate in the next chapter, it does not matter if the tongue sharing is literal or metaphorical; it will result in a change either way.

Chapter Two

BE CAREFUL WITH ME

Education, Sexual Violence, and Pleasure

[M]y pussy popping like grease in frying pan.
—SAPPHIRE, *PUSH* (1996)

Critics Aliyyah Abdur-Rahman and Candice Jenkins call attention
to the idea that, historically, due to stereotypes perpetuated by the
institution of slavery, essentially all Black relationships are thought
to be "queer," marked by delinquencies ranging from homosexuality,
unrestrained sexualities, promiscuity, hyberlibidinousness, incest,
violence, and all manner of sexual savagery.[1] More specifically, Abdur-
Rahman suggests that any relationship that cannot be identified as
heteronormatively white has been thought to be perverse. However,
this chapter illustrates that Celie and Shug's relationship in Alice
Walker's *The Color Purple* is the exact opposite of perverse; it is fundamental and necessary, as the two become literal manifestations of
Hurston's ideological tongue-sharing friends, problematizing patriarchy, religion, gender, and race norms while redefining and enhancing
Black womanhood for themselves and their community.

As has seemingly become the tradition when Black women display
unapologetic and time-sensitive truths in narrative form, Walker's 1982
novel won the Pulitzer Prize in 1983 and was banned from schools
in 1984. Her message was powerful and fast paced, so much so that
banishment seemed to be the only way to reduce its impact. Homosexuality, offensive language, and sexual explicitness were the supposed offenders, but ultimately, the text did not adhere to the politics
of respectability and illustrated the immense power that one can gain
from being self-identified, self-sexualized, and self-actualized. The

banishment did not prosper, however, as progressive Black women could not overlook the fact that Celie evolves from an illiterate child to a self-sufficient woman. Is this not the purpose of education?

Many educational institutions—whether primary, secondary, or postsecondary, public or private, religious or secular—have a stated mission of educating students so that they can become positive, active participants in the world. However, *The Color Purple* is an exemplar of attempts (by parents, churches, and institutions of learning) to ban or shield youth from engaging with many of the experiences they might encounter in the world. In a 2017 article titled "It's Non-Negotiable. We Have to Teach Social Justice in Our Schools," Professor Zachary Wright calls attention to J. Martin Rochester's claim that "schools ought to focus on the traditional curricula of reading, writing, mathematics, sciences, etc. [as opposed to] 'aspir[ing] to be churches or social work agencies.'" Wright retorts, "What this overlooks, however, is that education has always been political. When a nation has within its DNA laws regulating who can learn, with whom one can learn, and where one can learn, then the idea that a school ought not engage in the political realm reeks of forced naïveté." By making this argument, Wright acknowledges what authors such as Walker and Sapphire had already cognized: that the education system, like many systems of power, has traditionally discriminated against and further marginalized already marginalized groups. And the fact that lawmakers and policy makers, and even parents, prioritize traditional education over any others, namely education in one's own identity or sexuality, is precisely the reason why potential Winters procure dick-sucking lessons from teenagers when their mothers are at work, precisely why potential Celies cannot articulate the inappropriateness of sex acts performed on them by their parents, and precisely why young girls, like Roxane Gay in her younger years, attempt to eat themselves invisible after being raped. As insisted by Robert Kelly's former backup singer and dancer Jovante Cunningham, when those educational and supportive components are missing, the abused often see silent cries as their only option: "We're grown girls, but we are still little girls who cry silently."

To be clear, I am not suggesting that sexual violence and rape will cease simply because nontraditional forms of education are integrated into our educational systems. I am arguing that the rates of sexual violence will decrease because fewer women will place themselves in knowingly unhealthy and unsafe situations, they will be more confident in speaking up against those attempting to harm them, and those who do, unfortunately, still encounter sexual violence, will develop healthier means of coping. In other words, they will know that silence, self-harm, or harm against others are not the best or only solutions. Leaning on the shoulders of maverick feminists, uniting with other survivors, practicing numerous forms of self-care, reading, writing, and/or speaking, and seeking professional help are but a few options. When nontraditional education is not prioritized, though, these options are often completely foreign to victims of sexual violence. Therefore, it is incumbent on those who oppose nontraditional education and those who propose bans on texts such as *The Color Purple* to question the types of futures children, specifically young Black girls, will have if life is presented to them as something that should not be lived out, enjoyed, or spoken about, if they are left to stew alone with their trauma and shame, if they do not have allies.

Alice Walker, Sapphire, and Roxane Gay, I suggest, strongly considered these questions and used their texts to combat this lack of joy, community, healing, and progression. Walker makes note that in the literary world, "the life we save is our own" (*In Search* 14). This lifesaving endeavor can be taken literally as *The Color Purple*, as well as Sapphire's *PUSH* and Gay's *Hunger*, can be viewed as a form of activism with a fundamental objective of making certain that violence against Black women is recognized, reduced, punished, and, ultimately, eradicated. This stance is especially important in today's society, particularly among Black women, as the US Department of Justice's Office for Victims of Crime acknowledged in a 2018 report on intimate partner violence that, with the exception of Native American women, Black women face higher rates of domestic violence than women of any other race. Oftentimes, like the abuse experienced by Roxane Gay as well as the fictionalized characters of Celie and Precious, assaults go unreported initially, and other women, reactively, make it their duty and responsibility to advocate for the victims after the fact.

The cases of countless girls and women who fell prey to the infamous, once beloved pop star Robert Kelly is a prime example; many of the survivors suffered in silence until they were certain that they had the allyship and support of individuals and activist groups—namely dream hampton and the #MeToo and #MuteRKelly movements— that worked and are still working tirelessly to ascertain that not only R. Kelly but other victimizers like him as well are convicted and that centuries of abuse and violence inflicted on Black women and other women of color ceases. In *Reconstructing Womanhood: The Emergence of the Afro-American Woman Novelist* (1987), Hazel V. Carby declares:

> The institutionalized rape of black women has never been as powerful a symbol of black oppression as the spectacle of lynching. Rape has always involved patriarchal notions of women being, at best, not entirely unwilling accomplices, if not outwardly inviting a sexual attack. The links between black women and illicit sexuality consolidated during the antebellum years had powerful ideological consequences for the next hundred and fifty years. (39)

Essentially, in combating the violence inflicted on us by others, we must stop doing violence to one another. We must teach and encourage Black girls and women to envision and live in a world where silence is not their first or only option and being self-identified, self-sexualized, and self-actualized is the new norm.

On the whole, this chapter acknowledges that pleasure, as well as education, can be obtained in numerous ways. Even more, it acknowledges that those who are lacking in sensual education and find themselves on the receiving end of others' psychotic pleasures often find alternate, unhealthy means of coping, either through silence or other forms of abuse enacted on themselves; take Gay's gluttonous mutilation of her own body for instance. Many sixteenth- and seventeenth-century European travelers were allegedly searching for choice foods and other goods when they happened upon African women whom they abused and sought pleasure in. Even more, as noted in the Netflix series *High on the Hog: How African American Cuisine Transformed American* (2021), the refusal of food is the only means of power that captured Africans had as they were transported on ships from their homelands to America. So, this violent relationship with food, sex, pleasure, and power is historical and is, therefore, central to the analyses conducted in this chapter.

Like their ancestors before them, the protagonists in *The Color Purple* and *PUSH* have their bodies violently devoured by predators who forcefully isolate them and leave them to develop a complicated relationship with food, as well as a distaste for their own bodies and sexualities. It is not until they are reacquainted with society and are able to share their trauma with self-identified, self-actualized, and self-sexualized women (or those in progress) that they learn that their bodies and pleasures are natural, not shameful. Though they are not fully self-identified and self-actualized characters by the end of their respective novels, Celie and Precious, with the aid of their feminist mentors—the women with whom they form intentional sisterhoods—learn that 1) education is freedom, 2) sexuality is an undeniable part of one's identity (to be regarded but not valued over everything else), 3) the acceptance of this reality potentially results in greater control over, or greater pleasure received from, one's own sexual expressions and lived experiences, and 4) intentional sisterhoods and/or intergenerational relationships are a necessary component of positive, resilient, progressive, thriving, Black womanhood. More clearly, the analyses of *The Color Purple* and *PUSH* illustrate how the protagonists represent the respective author's dream of relinquishing the Black woman from centuries-old strongholds of food, sexual violence, and a lack of knowledge, while Roxane Gay's *Hunger: A Memoir of (My) Body* serves as a real-life depiction of how strong, powerful, and detrimental these strongholds can truly be.

THE PROBLEMS WITH CENSORSHIP: SEXUALITY IN FILM VERSUS FICTION

Author and music critic Amiri Baraka (1963) states, "An A flat played twice on the same saxophone by two different men does not have to sound the same" (194). In other words, art is highly subjective. This argument is particularly evident when the two "men" are from different racial, class, and gender backgrounds. Thus, it is not so surprising when film directors (a male-dominated occupation) get some things "wrong" in the process of adapting fiction, specifically Black women's fiction, to film. Directors inherently incorporate themselves into the work, and they also have a reputation to uphold that is slightly different from that of the original author. They, therefore, adhere to personal guidelines to make certain that their supportive viewers continue to come back. Additional characters and scenes are often added for a desired effect, yet the characters and scenes in the novel that do not make it to the big screen are most telling.

Often, but specifically in *The Color Purple* and *Precious*, the scenes hidden from public view are those involving sexuality and its importance to the development of a character, along with scenes that display a less than happy or "appropriate" ending. These deleted scenes, I argue, are the equivalent of the bans enacted in classrooms and libraries across the world. And a close examination of how other forms of art depict the lives of Black women characters that become self-identified in literary narratives invigorates critical conversations on Black female sexualities and further reiterates the fact that sexuality is an undeniable part of a realized and accomplished life. In this case specifically, the novels' protagonists, as a direct result of their explicit, intimate experiences and engagements with others, become significantly more complicated and self-identified characters than their film counterparts.

The fact that films tend to reach a wider audience than books seems to suggest that the message of the book/author will be propelled and magnified through the film. However, when pertinent parts of the narrative are omitted or distorted, the wrong message, or at least a message unintended by the original author, has the tendency to diminish the advocacy and progression envisioned by said author. More specifically, while *The Color Purple* the movie may have reached significantly more people than *The Color Purple* the novel, those who only see the film miss an important lesson on Black female communities, Black female sexualities, and Black womanhood.

Both *The Color Purple* and *PUSH* (*Precious*) gained attention and notoriety after the production of the motion pictures based on the novels. After the release of *The Color Purple* in December 1985, Tony Brown (1986) criticized the film and compared it to *The Birth of a Nation*, suggesting that it was racist, emasculating, and anti-Black family. Other Black male critics, namely Ishmael Reed, were in agreement. Some reviewers of the film version of *The Color Purple* were not pleased with the fact that a white male director was chosen to relay the narrative of a Black woman, but they were assured that it was Steven Spielberg's mere interest in the film that allowed for its production, as the Black woman's story had otherwise been overlooked. If the Black woman's story had been depicted in films prior to *The Color Purple*, the character was often a maid or some other stereotypical character. Walker had anticipated the backlash she would receive from the film, but as an activist concerned with saving her own life (i.e., saving the lives of Black women), she insists that she sold the screen rights because she wanted unlikely readers of the book to see the film and be exposed to the critical message in the narrative. In other words, Walker acknowledges the importance of the message leaving the academy and reaching the streets. She acknowledges the role that media plays in disseminating messages and propelling one's agenda. The novel's goal was to inform Black women of the possibility that a naïve, illiterate, victimized, young, Black girl can evolve and develop into an independent woman through sisterhood and self-fulfillment. However, as a result of the scenes added and deleted by the film's director, Celie's independence is not quite realized.

With a similar critical message and a similar desire to affect change, Sapphire sold the screen rights for *PUSH* because she wanted to "show this diseased situation with the hope that we can see it as something that needs to be healed as opposed to something that we need to hide from the public's view." She also goes on to express that Lee Daniels—not a white male director but a man nonetheless—was chosen over other potential directors because "he had gone over the edge in some cases with his own work . . . I felt this would be someone who would not back up from the material and would present something true and vital to the public" ("Sapphire's Story"). The 2009 release of the film and Daniels's seeming ability to "not back up" sparked similar responses from critics as *The Color Purple*, as *Precious* was also compared to *The Birth of a Nation* because of its treatment of Black family life. However, Pearl Cleage supported Sapphire's and Daniels's boldness, suggesting that the presentation of Black art is not about "putting our best face forward" and insisting that we "go beyond talking about the images and talk about the issues" (qtd. in Wellington 26). In a like manner, I stress the urgent need for African Americans to move beyond respectability and instead engage in more critical discussions about, as well as work to resolve, the systems from which the issues stem.

SPIELBERG'S DEDICATION TO
PATRIARCHY IN THE COLOR PURPLE

Attentive scholars have begun discussing the issues and have noted the additions made to the films *The Color Purple* and *Precious*, respectively, as well as the effects of the additions on the author's original narrative purpose. In response to Spielberg's *The Color Purple*, Molly Hite (1990) notes that Spielberg "reinscribed Mr. _____ (whom he named simply Mister, so that the title of authority became this character's identity) at the center of the story." Additionally, she suggests, "Spielberg went on to reinscribe the law of the father exactly where Walker had effaced it, by providing Shug with a textually gratuitous 'daddy' who is also a preacher and thus the representative of the Christian white father-God explicitly repudiated in the passage that gives the book its title" (440). In sum, by centering respectability (through the inclusion of this God-like representative) and masculinity (through the renaming of Mr. _____), Spielberg effectively decenters Celie and egregiously takes away the modicum of power Walker had permitted her.

Walker's initial naming and spelling of Mr. _____, specifically the blank space, recalls a void in naming that can be filled by any man, making him far from honorable, but instead dispensable. In addition, the naming seems to be a play on the secrecy forced on Celie by her stepfather, as all men she comes in contact with, with the exception of Harpo, Jack, and Grady, are simply referred to as Mr. _____ or Rev. Mr. _____. Harpo, Jack, and Grady are portrayed as quiet, supportive, and somewhat effeminate men and, therefore, nonthreatening to Celie or any other woman. Thus, their characters are respected rather than feared and their names revealed. Overall, whereas Walker's original spelling may have left room for Celie to exhibit politeness and discretion, the renaming in the film requires her to be submissive, and unending submission to Mister in the film does not allow for the eventual freedom she attains from Mr. _____ in the novel.

Furthermore, the fact that Shug's dead father (in the novel) comes to life (in the film) to forgive her of her sins and welcome her back to his fold in one of the closing scenes is indeed striking, especially since this forgiveness and welcome is the exact opposite of what Shug suggests she needs in the novel. While meeting with an adult son she left to be raised by her parents, Walker's Shug acknowledges that she had traditional parents who did not approve of her sensual way of life and insists that "they had a lot of love to give. But I needed love plus understanding. They run a little short of that" (273). Before talking with her son, Shug is unaware that her parents had "*been* dead" for nine or ten years, and she confesses, "You know I never think bout mama and daddy. You know how tough I think I is" (273; emphasis original). Yet, the film takes away a great deal of Shug's toughness, as her father is frequently brought to her mind and the minds of movie watchers; he can regularly be found perched on a pulpit preaching damnation against the very acts his daughter is committing. His constant rejection burdens her, and in the end, he is not required to have the understanding that Shug (of the novel) hoped for because she changes her life to please him. This is respectability at its peak, and it is forced on Walker's character by Spielberg.

Even more, the fact that Spielberg's desire for a happy, respectable ending did not necessitate the resurrection of both parents is clearly misogynistic and a testimony to the overall lack of significance society places on the lives of Black women—as if satisfying a man (even a father) is one's ultimate goal.[2] Ironically, though Shug's sisterhood and relationship is what helps to free Celie, in Spielberg's depiction, her own freedom lies in the hands of a man. This male-controlled freedom exists because Shug is originally depicted as a strong, self-identified, self-sexualized, and self-actualized woman, characteristics that naturally seem to require redress and forgiveness.

As noted in the above two variances, when Spielberg has the theoretical saxophone, many notes in *The Color Purple* sound and look differently. Other added scenes include, but are not limited to, his allowing Celie to hold her daughter when she meets Corrine in the store, Celie and Nettie's spelling dialogue before Nettie is kicked off Mr. _____'s property, Mr. _____'s failed attempt at cooking Shug breakfast when she is first brought to the place, a brawl between the men at Harpo's juke joint after Sophia knocks out Squeak, Mr. _____ slapping Celie after catching her reading Nettie's letters, and an all-around repentance of sin in the final scene. As Hite noted, the majority of these additions bring Mr. _____ (and men in general) to the center of the film and reduce Celie to the ignorant maid trope from which Walker had tried to liberate her (and Black women). Ultimately, Spielberg does to Celie what so many white authors do to their Black characters: he controls her and limits her sexual development under the guise of allowing her to tell her own story of growth. Spielberg seems unaware of the inherent difficulty to grow and fully develop as a woman without understanding all aspects of womanhood, including a fully realized sexuality. Or perhaps he was very much aware, but rather chose to focus on more fully developing or more positively portraying his white manhood instead.

In an interview with *Show Biz* (1985), Spielberg suggests that he "never really looked upon [the film] as just a black movie" and admits that he "made the book personal . . . wanted part of it to belong to [him]" ("Steven Spielberg"). Whether Spielberg saw the text as a racial one or not, it is very unlikely that a malleable item belonging to a Black woman will look and feel the same after it has been possessed and used by a white man. This is precisely why there are traditionally patriarchal additions in the film. Equally so, there are deleted or *white*washed scenes that would have clearly centralized Celie and illustrated her growth as an independent woman who is aware of and confident in her sexuality, as opposed to depicting her as the perpetually naïve, fearful, underdeveloped character movie viewers see. These viewers are not permitted to see Celie's initial abuse by her stepfather; conversely, they are not privy to the sisterhood shown to Celie by Mr. _____'s sisters when they come over to lavish Celie with compliments and force Mr. _____ to buy her new clothes. Likewise, Celie's interaction with Shug when she cooks her the tempting ham-centered breakfast and her time in Memphis, Tennessee, where she is introduced to different viewpoints and cultures, are also omitted from the film. Of course, it is impossible to include in a film each scene from a book, but oddly, Spielberg seems to have added as many scenes as he deleted, and the film runs for over two and a half hours. Surely some of these pertinent scenes could have been included.

Two other very significant scenes, both involving some instance of sex (read rape) or sexuality, are also omitted from the film. Needless to say, during the year 1985, society was not as comfortable with sexuality as it is becoming in this twenty-first century, and even current-day rhetoric and politics surrounding sexuality are flawed. Nevertheless, there were mainstream films produced even in 1985 that involved conspicuous nudity and sex. However, very few involved lesbianism among Black women or sex between Black couples in general, and Spielberg seemed not to want to change this depiction because then it would not be "a part of him."

One significant omission involves a secondary or seemingly insignificant character, Squeak. Although she is a secondary character, Squeak's development is parallel to and affects the development of the protagonist because a critical message of this narrative is the significance of Black sisterhoods. In the novel, after Sofia is beaten and jailed by white men, her family develops a plan to appeal to the white warden on terms that white men have been historically known to admire and exploit. They tempt him with a well-dressed mulatto woman, hoping that her innocuous voice and alluring presence, in addition to the fact that she is ultimately a part of "his family," would sway him into releasing Sofia. The plan both works and backfires when the white warden does what powerful white men have historically been known to do to attractive, powerless Black women. He rapes Squeak and releases Sofia from jail. This scene, and ultimately this white man, is deleted from the movie because he is too reminiscent of countless real-life white men in ante- or postbellum history, and since Spielberg (a white man) has made this his personal tale, this history, and therefore this man, no longer exists and is best left hidden from movie viewers. Is this Spielberg's attempt at revisionist history? In the narrative by Alice Walker, a Black woman, "Poor little Squeak come home with a limp. Her dress rip. Her hat missing and one of the heels come off her shoe . . . He saw the Hodges in me, she say. And didn't like it one bit . . . He say if he was my uncle he wouldn't do it to me. That be a sin. But this just little fornication. Everybody guilty of that—" everybody except Spielberg and the potential white ancestors he is trying to protect, that is (97–98). Essentially, he counteracts Walker's protest with his own. Spielberg's revision is the equivalent of screaming "All Lives Matter" following cries that "Black Lives Matter," as the marginalized are sidelined even further when those in power take up additional space to *re-center* themselves.

Oprah Winfrey, who plays Sofia in the film, defends her director, stating, "Spielberg said he couldn't include every incident, and that if he had, the film would've been too depressing. As it is, it's a joyous picture, a triumphant one. The essence and spirit of the book are there and that's most important" (qtd. in Rice). While the above deleted scene is undoubtedly "depressing," it precisely depicts the essence of the story. After this incident, Squeak, otherwise quiet and timid, gains her voice and asserts herself as "Mary Agnes," which in turn affects Celie, since it is the community of strong women that ultimately encourages and nurtures one another. In the novel, Squeak's newly developed voice and assertions give way to Celie's, so without this incident in the film, Celie is not the vocal, self-identified woman readers find near the end of Walker's narrative.

Furthermore, Shug is definitely important to Celie's growth as a self-sexualized woman. She introduces Celie to her clitoris, the powerful "button" that Spielberg never introduces to movie viewers. As such, he leaves Celie powerless. Although Spielberg allows Shug and Celie to engage in a friendly kiss, it is watered down and looks very innocent, or comical even, as opposed to romantic. He treats the interaction as if Shug is simply building up a torn-down sister (which she is), but Shug is also gaining pleasure from Celie's affection and companionship and teaching Celie the significance of pleasure as well. In the novel, Shug shows Celie how to enjoy herself during moments of intimacy and how to depend solely on herself for enjoyment. Shug questions, "What, too shame even to go off and look at yourself? . . . All dressed up for Harpo's and scared to look at your own pussy." After much hesitation, Celie finally looks and discovers that her "pussy lips be black" but the "inside look like a wet rose." Then, she states, "I look at her and touch it with my finger. A little shiver go through me. Nothing much. But just enough to tell me this the right button to mash" (78).

In learning about this sensual part of herself, Celie sparks what eventually becomes her independence from Mr. _____ and anyone who may have once had control over her, including Shug. In fact, in a scene where Shug and Mr. _____ are being intimate, Celie "pull[s] the quilt over [her] head and finger[s her] little button and titties . . ." (80). Where is this freedom in the film? Representing both a form of self-consolation and self-empowerment, perhaps this kind of self-pleasure, this Black female independence, was too much for the white male Spielberg (and his audience) to fathom or tolerate. But why? Easy. Black women have, for centuries, been the mules of the world, used and abused by white and Black men alike; the thought of Black women taking reign over their own lives and bodies seems to suggest less power for their oppressors and therefore seems to threaten and redefine traditional definitions and expectations of manhood. And herein lies the problem with patriarchy and respectability politics: one person's freedom should not be dependent on another's imprisonment and vice versa.

Nonetheless, so much of Celie's story is left untold, and Spielberg's film brings to life the popular quote, "Believe only half of what you see." All the same, the film, read in conjunction with the novel, fortifies the discussion on Black female sexualities, as the choices made in the film adaptation bring to life Walker's underlying argument, that Black sisterhood is an essential component of advocacy and progression because society fears self-identified, self-sexualized, and self-actualized Black women. Because of Spielberg's apparent fear, audiences of the film alone may not be aware that the self-sexualized Celie knows she "can live content without Shug" and that she turns down a proposal from Mr. _____, "who done ast [her] to marry him again, this time in the spirit as well as in the flesh" (288). These revelations at the end of the novel are the essence of her independence, an independence not afforded Celie in the film.

Ultimately, Spielberg's choice to add scenes that are less woman-centered and delete scenes that demonstrate the magnitude of Celie's sexuality reduces the strength of his protagonist, as Walker's novel (and others analyzed in this project) clearly indicates that sexuality is an undeniable part of one's identity. The acceptance of this fact, along with encounters with self-identified, self-sexualized, and self-actualized individuals—or maverick feminists—can potentially allow for one's mental and spiritual growth, as well as the possibility of self-governance and self-fulfillment, characteristics Walker's Celie possesses but Spielberg's Celie does not fully realize.

DANIELS'S FORCED HAPPY ENDINGS

In comparison to Spielberg's, Lee Daniels's adaptation is truer to original form, perhaps partially because Daniels's saxophone, although masculine, is Black. Still, attentive critics notice the modifications in his work as well. In reference to the film *Precious*, which was renamed altogether from the original title *PUSH*, Christopher Burrell and James Wermers (2012) insist that "Daniels's film is not a valuable tool for elucidating or engaging Sapphire's novel, as the film is far too reductive to capture the novel's richness . . . [but] *Precious* can, in fact, be an effective teaching tool for engaging a number of issues that are important to the novel and in contemporary society" (212).

Indeed, Daniels's adaptation, like Spielberg's, includes added, deleted, and modified scenes, so it is no substitute for the novel. Daniels seems to have hoped that his additions would add a bit of *light* to what otherwise would have been a dark movie. For instance, Ms. Rain is now light skinned, and a light-skinned male nurse, too, acts as somewhat of a savior figure for Precious. In addition to these fair-skinned characters who highlight the issue of colorism in Black society, Daniels's adaptation also includes a young girl, Ruby, whom Precious pushes around and ignores for a great portion of the movie before finally making her feel loved and appreciated at the end of the film. Also, Precious's mother, Mary, has an interesting love for cats and owns multiple. How do these additions add light to the story? The teacher and nurse appear to be less threatening and, therefore, tenderer, while Mary seemingly cares for something even if she does not care for her daughter, and Precious stands in solidarity with a fellow neglected Black daughter when she finally "sees" Ruby. Unfortunately, the addition of all of this light seems to have left little room for Precious's character to develop to her full potential.

Specifically, because of the film's fixation on stereotypes and audience appeal, Daniels's viewers are not aware of Precious's close relationship with fellow "Each One Teach One" peer Rita Romero. In the novel, Rita, a Puerto Rican, is depicted as a former drug addict and high school dropout who *does* mothering well. During one of the class exercises, Ms. Rain asks each student what she does well, and Rita's response is that she is a good mother. Being a good parent is very important to her because she became an orphan after watching her father murder her mother. As an orphan, Rita became a victim of rape, worked as a prostitute, and eventually contracted HIV. Few would consider Rita a role model, but as previously mentioned, the concept of the role model is flawed, and Rita's past does not diminish her ability to provide inspiration and support to others. In fact, in Sapphire's *PUSH*, Rita is Precious's link to wholeness and healing because she embodies two important characteristics of maverick feminists. Although very much still in progress herself, Rita is self-identified (as indicated above) and understands the importance of sisterhood, particularly when one is working through personal traumas.

In Daniels's film adaptation, though, other than her introduction to the class at the beginning of the term and a slip at the museum that causes her to grab Precious's hand for balance, Rita is barely a visible or memorable character. The omission of Rita as a significant character affects the magnitude to which Precious learns to speak and be heard, her eventual assertion as a subject as opposed to an object, and the extent to which she questions her own sexuality and intimate engagements. Specifically, in the novel, Rita is part of the reason Precious is able to continue to *push* after Mary tells Precious that her father has died of AIDS. Rita escorts Precious to Incest Survivor meetings, treats her to meals, and is depicted as a true friend.[3] With her, Precious is able to ride buses and see parts of New York she had not been previously familiar with. For the protagonist, these trips have a similar impact as Celie's stay in Memphis, as Precious learns that New York, and the world, are much larger than Harlem; her worldview is expanded in a way that movie Precious's is not.

Additionally, at the first Incest Survivor meeting, Precious is initially in a daze, afraid to tell her story until she realizes that Rita supports her; she states, "Someone is holding my hand. It's Rita, She is massage my hand. I come back from being a bird . . ." (129). This supportive touch is far different from the accidental clasp Rita gives Precious in the movie, and this is not their only physical interaction in the novel. Immediately after the meeting, Rita and Precious go "out for coffee," and Rita puts her arm around Precious's shoulder as a sign of support while she is ordering because this is another first for Precious (130). She also hugs Precious, and Precious states, "I like how Rita is, she know the world, how to act and stuff. Sometimes I don't have a clue!" (131). The exposure Precious (of the novel) gets from being with Rita helps her realize her lack of knowledge, whereas in the movie, it seems okay for Precious to have no clue about the world. More importantly, when Daniels has the metaphorical saxophone, Precious's incest survival does not have as great a significance because although a joke is made about "incest" versus "insect," filmic Precious never even attends the Incest Survivor meetings in order to have this interaction with Rita, and the joke is clearly incorporated again to add light and humor to a serious issue. Needless to say, people experiencing situations such as Precious's would hardly see the acknowledgment of the meetings via a short joke as a replacement for the actual meetings themselves, as there is no substitute for healing. In effect, film Precious is denied healing in two forms: traditional healing through therapy and maverick feminist healing via a positive sisterhood.

In essence, while Precious is indeed the narrator of the film and tells her story to audience members, the film portrays her as someone to be looked at as opposed to someone to be listened to. She does not get the opportunity in the film to share her story with people who understand and have experienced similar events and traumas. Similarly, she does not *push* and is simply *Precious*, no longer invisible but still not heard. The change of title is a clear indication of Precious's lack of action. In the novel, after gaining comfort from Rita's massage, when Precious raises her hand at the Incest Survivor meeting to tell her story, she equates it to "going up through the smell of Mama, my hand is pushing Daddy's dick out my face" (130). She does not have this privilege in the movie and, therefore, is yet susceptible to the internal, if not physical, effects of her parents' actions. Simply put, in the film, even after her father's death, his dick is still in Precious's face, holding her back from life and healing. Ultimately, Precious experiences several firsts with Rita, and they are not significantly noted in the film, perhaps because Rita, overall, does not stand out to audiences as one to offer assistance or guidance, because she is not "respectable." It is virtually impossible, though, to adhere to respectability politics when one's youth is overshadowed by trauma that goes unacknowledged, undiscussed, and untreated.

Despite Rita's social status, these firsts with Rita aid Precious in being dependent on herself just as Shug's introduction of firsts to Celie aids Celie in being dependent on herself. Without Rita, Precious might still be controlled by her daddy's dick and have no clue about life or her own personal desires. Daniels, like the proponents of book bans, seemed to think that involvement in the classroom/alternative school would be sufficient enough education to aid in Precious's healing and progression. However, the education that one gains from being attached to and supported by a community of self-identified, self-sexualized, and/or self-actualized individuals is equally important, if not more important.

In the novel, Rita is Precious's immediate example of strength: a single, HIV-infected mother like herself, who is strong and continues a "normal" life with a normal boyfriend. Precious states, "Rita got man. Rhonda God. Ms. Rain a fren. Jermaine say hole worl her lovr" (102). Who does Precious have? More specifically, who does Precious want? She states that she "GOT frens," but she also contemplates what it would be like to "have sex wif a kute coot boy thas [her] own age" (102). Because sexuality is an undeniably powerful aspect of one's being, Precious, although traumatized by sex (due to rape), does not inwardly repress her desires to experience pleasure in a positive way. She does outwardly repress these feelings, however; knowing that society places such a great stigma on expressed sexuality, she feels ashamed and embarrassed and does not want her teacher, whom she shares almost everything else with, to know her desires.

Despite Precious's longings for intimacy and pleasure, however, Sapphire makes it clear in several interviews that she had no intentions of giving Precious a happy ending, specifically not a boyfriend. This lack of male companion is a trend in the finale of each of the primary texts previously discussed because a sense of self and a

community of female supporters take precedence over male companionship. Daniels, likewise, does not see fit to allow Precious to express
her sexuality with a "kute coot boy" her own age, but he does attempt to
give her a happy ending. In the final movie scenes, audience members
see Precious taking Abdul swimming, and they see her walk away from
the social services building with Abdul on her side and Little Mongo in
tow. In the novel, however, she only takes on responsibility for Abdul
because Mongo is in a mental institution. Sapphire's Precious states,
"They put her institution, say she severely (mean real) retarded, and
Toosie hadn't been doing things that would help her—Like colors on
wall and books 'n shit, so she really in bad shape. They say even if she
could be help, take a lot more than me to help, and ain't I got a full load
with Abdul. Anyway . . ." (84). Throughout the book, Toosie, Precious's
grandmother, is noted as Mongo's caretaker, although Mary actually
receives welfare assistance for her. With the realization that she really
can't save Mongo, Sapphire's Precious brushes the idea off, hence the
word "anyway." Black families are not depicted in a particularly positive
light in either the novel or the film, but by permitting Precious to take
responsibility for both children, Daniels paints her as a better parent
than her mother and grandmother, suggesting that she might appear
more *respectable* and empathetic if she takes care of her responsibilities as a parent. However, by taking care of her responsibilities and
being respectable, even though "it take a lot more than me to help,"
Daniels's protagonist neglects her own needs and progression, remains
somewhat stagnant, and perhaps causes more harm than good.

Overall, as opposed to making certain that the protagonist herself
is well developed, Daniels's depiction seems more concerned with de-
livering an image the audience can tolerate. Thus, Precious, like Celie
in the ending that critics, including Sapphire, condemn, is reunited
with her children and thought to live happily ever after. This happiness, however, is situational because although Precious is a victim
of sexual abuse and has subsequently contracted a sexual disease,
Daniels, as a result of diminishing Precious's relationship with Rita,
does not allow her the opportunity to even attempt to become self-
identified, self-sexualized, or self-actualized.

To be clear, I am well aware that the two films under discussion, *The
Color Purple* and *Precious*, had screenwriters who were responsible

for developing the scripts for the movies, but under the control and management of directors Spielberg and Daniels, the movies greatly missed the mark. The films undoubtedly address sensitive issues and depict graphic scenes that were not typically being addressed and depicted by other directors during the times of the films' respective productions, but added and deleted scenes that work to make the films more positive and tolerable, likewise, hinder character development. In each case, an otherwise complex image is reduced to a stereotype. Indeed, while Daniels seemingly did a better job than Spielberg of "sticking to the script," they both, clearly, had their own personal investments; neither of these investments seemed to include the development of a self-identified, self-sexualized, and self-actualized Black woman.

FINGER LICKIN' GOOD: FOOD AND SEXUALITY'S CONNECTIONS TO PLEASURE AND PAIN

In the seminal collection of nonfiction *In Search of Our Mothers' Gardens* (1983), Alice Walker explores racial politics, literary ostracism and longevity, motherhood, childhood, and many other aspects of feminism relating to the beauty and complexity of the Black female mind and body. Noting that Black female sexuality is often disregarded by white feminists, Walker states, "To think of black women as women is impossible if you cannot imagine them with vaginas." These vaginas, she insists, are "the color of raspberries and blackberries—of scuppernongs and muscadines—and of that strong, silvery sweetness, with, as well, a sharp flavor of salt" (383). According to this logic, the Black vagina is much like the Black race in general; it comes in an array of shades and can be both sweet and salty, or pleasant and disagreeable. It is no secret that many Black vaginas, in all their beauty and flavor, however, serve as sites of turmoil, tragedy, and trepidation. *The Color Purple* and *PUSH* protagonists, Celie and Precious respectively, at an early age, endure physical and sexual abuse from parental figures that cause trauma to and ultimately influence how the daughters view their own vaginas. Although food is often used as an escape in the novels, raspberries and blackberries, particularly, are the furthest images from Celie's and Precious's minds as they are trampled on by their father and husband, and mother and father, respectively.

Noting the power and ecstasy of food, in his self-help book titled *Oprah, In Her Words, Our American Princess* (2008), Tuchy Palmieri quotes the noted godmother of the film *Precious*, stating, "My idea of heaven is a great big baked potato and someone to share it with" (47). As mentioned previously, food and companionship, whether cordial or violent, have been interconnected in Black communities for an immense amount of time. African Americans tend to commemorate almost every significant event with a feast—weddings, funerals, birthdays, or Saturdays. Barbecuing, a tradition practiced by Africans before their arrival to America, is specifically prevalent in Black communities; chicken, beef, and pork are favorites at barbecues. Noting that the barbecue is "always inherently political," culinary historian Michael Twitty suggests that "highly spicing meats . . . the use of the wooden grill framework, the slow cooking process . . . and the social context of barbeque . . . hearken back to the culture's African roots . . . it was enslaved Africans and their descendants who became heir to multiple traditions and in turn incorporated those traditions into a standard repertoire known as Southern barbeque." The barbecue is noted as a communal event; many bonds are formed, strengthened, and sometimes even weakened over these feasts, as they usually require intimacy among the people in attendance.

Dubbed BBQ Becky, a white Oakland woman in April 2018 knew all too well the communal healing and strength that can accompany a Black barbecue/feast, and like the opponents of *The Color Purple*, knew no other way to reduce its power but by banishing it, by calling the police. The internet, specifically Black Twitter, in its truest form, ripped BBQ Becky to shreds, and of course, as Brittney Cooper would say, she shed white girl tears. However, the most intriguing result of this incident is the grander scale of communal strength that followed in that same Oakland park several weeks after. Hundreds of Black people gathered, barbecued, played music, and danced, and fire marshals and police officers attended to show support. This event, a form of activism and pride, demonstrated that there is strength in numbers. But would this display of strength and pride have occurred if it were not for the internet, if it were not for progressive, unapologetic, young (and old) innovators who believe that self-respect outweighs respectability?

In a manner similar to those that BBQ Becky hoped to abolish, many of the meals and feasts described in Walker's *The Color Purple* and Sapphire's *PUSH* yield an illusory or trancelike intimacy between those in attendance. The culinary gatherings and meals depicted in the two works are a demonstration that food is indeed political, promotes community, has a tendency to influence vulnerability, and, ultimately, is interconnected with sexuality. Like the enslavers who tried to control their captured with food, the characters in *The Color Purple* and *PUSH* often use the enticement of food to gain intimacy in order to transport themselves to an ephemeral heaven on earth; even the often-victimized Celie is guilty of this deceptive deed.

At the conclusions of *The Color Purple* and *PUSH*, the two protagonists seem to conquer the obstacles once hampering their abilities to be "normal" operating citizens. Yet, because Celie and Precious are victims of abuse—verbal, physical, and especially sexual—throughout the majority of their narratives, readers may be unable to see them as agents in their own sexualities (movie watchers definitely won't be able to see it). Indeed, Celie is raped by her stepfather and recollects the beginning of the abuse as follows: "First he put his thing up gainst my hip and sort of wiggle it around. Then he grab hold of my titties. Then he push his thing inside my pussy. When that hurt, I cry. He start to choke me, saying You better shut up and git used to it. But I don't never git used to it" (1). This scene depicts an innocent, naïve girl who is molested and victimized during the first of many violent sexual encounters with the one man she may have looked to for protection. Each *then* or *when* denotes additional, compounded abuse. It is disheartening to think that someone can become accustomed to this type of assault and oppression, and Celie herself suggests that she "don't never git used to it," but the lack of sensual interaction, later, with her "husband," Mister, suggests that she does something closely akin to just that. With Mister, she literally goes with the flow. Celie maintains, "I lay there thinking about Nettie while he on top of me, wonder if she safe. And then I think bout Shug Avery. I know what he doing to me he done to Shug Avery and maybe she like it" (12). The two passages together indeed indicate that despite telling her own story, Celie has many things done to her and is the object of someone else's actions very regularly in her narrative. However, this indication is not completely suggestive of Celie's control over her own sexuality. As sexuality is often interconnected with food in this novel, readers can observe that Celie knows the power of both and thus uses food to instigate a physical and emotional bond between herself and Shug. Essentially, although Celie lacks formal education and is not self-actualized, in retrospect, she is definitely a "much more sophisticated character than [readers] are initially led to believe" (T. Harris 157).

After accepting the notion that she "sure *is* ugly" and, therefore, is outwardly undesired by "the most beautiful woman [she] ever saw," Celie lures Shug into a companionship by showering her with the feast that ultimately opens the figurative door for them to feast on one another in the future (46, emphasis original; 6). In other words, Celie's dream of becoming one with Shug comes true shortly after she entices Shug with food. Celie states, "I ast Shug Avery what she want for breakfast. She say, what yall got, I say ham, grits, eggs, biscuits, coffee, sweet milk or butter milk, flapjacks. Jelly and jam . . . I feel like something pushing me forward. If I don't watch out I'll have hold of her hand, tasting her fingers in my mouth . . . Nobody living can stand to smell cured ham without tasting it" (51–52). In this passage, the usually dormant Celie has to *repress* her feelings in order to avoid *pressing up* on Shug. Celie gives Shug more food options than she can handle in one sitting and, ultimately, and somewhat violently, equates Shug's body, her fingers specifically, to the food that is to be taken in and consumed. More importantly, however, Celie notes the power of the smell of cured ham, insisting that nobody alive can resist it.

The irresistible smell of the ham is comparable to the smell of the vagina's natural pheromones, which are "meant to attract a sexual partner" (Rankin 67). Moreover, the process of curing the ham, adding salt, sugar, and other chemicals that add flavor and a pink or reddish color to the meat, is not unlike the description of the Black vagina illustrated by Walker and mentioned in the first paragraph of this section. In addition, the vagina, in popular culture, is frequently referred to as a "ham wallet" because of the vagina's similar coloration (presumably taste and smell as well) to the meat, along with its ability to hold and contain *valuable* objects. Whether Walker was or was not aware of all of the different correlations between the first item of food on Celie's list and the actual female sexual organ Celie has yet to *feel* the intensity of, the depictions in the narrative highlight what is implicitly Celie's full awareness that food, specifically cured ham, makes one vulnerable.

Celie notes how the otherwise confident and bold Shug is intimidated by her culinary prowess and, like a hungry rodent, has fallen into her trap, stating, "I put my plate down on the card table by the bed. I go dip her up some water. I come back, pick up my plate. Look like a little mouse been nibbling the biscuit, a rat run off with the ham" (52). The plate *belongs* to Celie, and Shug soon will too, as her stature is now equivalent to a minute rodent, one that finds ham irresistible. Shortly after Shug and Celie's interaction at breakfast, Celie is helping to "scratch [songs] out of [Shug's] head"; they become practically inseparable, and Celie's food enticement encourages Shug to *open up* in multiple ways (53). Later in the novel, Celie notes how Shug "haul[s] off and kiss[es her] on the mouth"; then she "feels something real soft and wet on [her] breast, feel like one of [her] little lost babies mouth," a lost baby that is apparently *hungry*, but in this case, hungry for a type of pleasure that cannot be acquired from food (114–15). All in all, this example demonstrates that while Celie, in fact, is a victim of sexual abuse, she, too, realizes the sensual and intimate power of food. Her identity as a woman on the verge of becoming self-identified and self-sexualized may come later in the narrative, but this particular engagement with Shug suggests that while Celie is indeed a victim, not adhering to respectability politics, in this case, is a choice, as she desires a seemingly deviant type of pleasure and fulfillment not often supported by society. Her character is an acknowledgement that sexuality is complex and unavoidable and that pleasure is a natural desire, even if you are a woman who has been sexually abused for most of your life.

In an essay titled "Spiky Green Life: Environmental, Food, and Sexual Justice Themes in *PUSH*," Joni Adamson states, "*PUSH* illustrates that our bodies, like our communities and our homes, are our first environments, and that our bodies have been placed at risk, poisoned by toxins, by too much or not enough food, or even killed due to social and physical harms that may be exacerbated because of gender and sexuality" (85). In summation, Adamson's essay suggests that the body is a dwelling that should be kept clean, not simply by maintaining good hygiene, but by taking in healthy foods moderately as well; however, poverty-stricken communities such as those depicted in *PUSH* have little knowledge of or access to these healthy foods. The lack of proper nutrition and other necessities due to socioeconomic impediments leads to physical violence that further destroys the already improperly nourished body. This argument is significant because it highlights the multiple purposes and effects of food. It is not simply used for nutritional or sustenance purposes and, if abused, has side effects expanding beyond weight gain. Instead of using food to entice a lover, Precious is a victim of food abuse, but like Celie, she recognizes that the sensual body and food are deeply interconnected.

Throughout the novel, Precious has a propensity for using similes and metaphors. She unwittingly compares almost any unpleasant situation to a crude sex act. For instance, when she does not turn her math book to the correct page and is asked by the teacher, Mr. Wicher, to leave class, Precious disrupts the class and insists that she "ain' going nowhere mutherfucker till the bell ring." Her description of Mr. Wicher's reaction follows: "He look like a bitch just got a train pult on her. He don't know what to do" (5). In a similar situation, when she makes an unexpected comment to the guidance counselor, Precious notes, "She look at me like I said I wanna suck a dog's dick or some shit"; then, "Mrs Lichenstein look at me like I got three arms or a bad odor out my pussy or something" (7–8). When life's situations appear immoderate or unbearable, Precious compares them to sex acts. This is undoubtedly a result of how she experiences sex, in an uncomfortable and violent way. However, when sex acts themselves—particularly the rape and sexual abuse inflicted on her by her parents—are immoderate or unbearable, Precious compares them to food.

During the course of the novel, Precious narrates the details of many immoderate and unbearable sex acts carried out on her, but the most vivid of these depictions are connected to food. For example, it is understood that Precious's mother, Mary, sexually abuses her daughter to compensate for the fact that "Miz Claireece Precious Jones [is] fucking [her] husband . . . [and] he done quit [Mary]. He left [Mary] 'cause of [Precious]" (19). Yet, only one scene actually depicts this abuse. Mary uses food to intoxicate Precious and then fingers her daughter, or penetrates her digitally, while she is in a food-induced stupor. Precious describes this ghastly event by stating:

> I eat 'cause she say eat. I don't taste nothin' . . . Eating, first 'cause she make me, beat me if I don't, then eating hoping the pain in my neck go away. keep eating . . . and I just fall back on the couch so full it like I'm dyin' and I go to sleep like I always do; almost . . . I feel Mama's hand between my legs, moving up my thigh. Her hand stop, she getting ready to pinch me if I move. I just lay still still, keep my eyes close. I tell Mama's other hand between her legs now 'cause the smell fill the room. Mama can't fit into bathtub no more. Go sleep, go sleep, go *sleep*, I tells myself. Mama's hand creepy spider, up my legs, in my pussy. God please. Thank you god I say as I fall asleep. (20–21)

Although neither Walker's nor Sapphire's protagonist confesses to being a Christian, the God that Celie writes her earnest letters to is the God that Precious prays to when Mary is using Precious's food-filled body in an attempt to transport herself to a sensual *heaven*. The dinner that the two eat could likely serve a family of five, but Mary herself has a food addiction and forces Precious to eat so that she will become fat and hopefully undesirable to her "husband." The gross intake of food does not hinder Mary, but rather encourages her, to desire Precious herself. Not surprisingly, the two are having ham hocks for dinner, along with a spread of collard greens, corn bread, fried apple pies, and macaroni 'n cheese. Ham is a commonality between Celie's enticing breakfast and the intoxicating dinner prepared by Precious; however, as Adamson notes about the eating habits of those living in impoverished areas, Precious and Mary either prefer or could only afford the less expensive hock as opposed to the ham proper.[4] Nevertheless, the meal *fills* Precious up and makes her vulnerable to be *felt up* by her mother.

The correlation between food and sex(uality) becomes so apparent and distinct in Precious's life that when her body is used by others, even when she is not physically eating, she conjures up a dish. When she is pregnant with her second child, the "baby feels like a watermelon between [her] bones getting bigger" (57). Furthermore, she recollects instances of abuse at the hands of her father, describing the uncontrollable and unwarranted pleasure she feels, insisting that she "feel the hot sauce hot cha cha feeling when he be fucking [her]" and her "pussy popping like grease in frying pan" (58, 111). When her son is finally born, he devours her body as well, and Precious notes, "I feed Abdul. My body is his breakfast. I gotta get something to eat myself" (78). Although her body is a feast for others, because Precious has very few intimate companions, she herself is depicted as hungry throughout the novel. One particular instance is when she has no money for food and steals chicken from a diner (37). This hunger is both physical and mental, however, aspects that ultimately drive her to find fullness via alternative avenues, alternative education specifically. And the relationships Precious builds at the alternative school are influential in helping her, like Shug helped Celie, realize her own desires and gain a sense of physical, mental, and sexual autonomy.

In essence, these novels articulate that self-actualized Black female sexuality is both a prize and a weapon, and, as reasoned, food has the ability to strengthen or weaken it.[5] However, as Adamson's essay suggests, economic status plays a grand role in the food choices individuals make. Celie grows her own crops at her Georgia home, and Precious's mother receives welfare assistance, but the two are both on the lower end of the economic ladder. In fact, many will argue, and to a certain extent this analysis supports, that the economic standing of the two protagonists is directly related to their victimization. All the same, it is important to note, and literary works support, that food abuse and sexual abuse are common among those in higher economic classes as well, especially if the victim is not self-identified, self-sexualized, and/or self-actualized. Roxane Gay's memoir is testament to this likelihood.

FOR THERE IS NO RESPECT OF PERSONS WITH ABUSE AND TRAUMA, OR WHEN BEING A *GOOD* DAUGHTER IS NOT GOOD ENOUGH

For many years growing up, as reiterated very often throughout her memoir, *Hunger: A Memoir of (My) Body*, Roxane Gay struggled with respectability politics, what she calls being a good girl. She insists, "The only way I know of moving through the world is as a Haitian American, a Haitian daughter. A Haitian daughter is a good girl. She is respectful, studious, hard-working. She never forgets the importance of her heritage. We are part of the first free black nation in the Western Hemisphere" (55). Beholding these truths and recognizing the weight of being a Haitian daughter, Gay acknowledges that gender and race became a burden early in her life. Her upbringing was decidedly different from the fictional characters Celie and Precious; she grew up in a loving, wealthy, two-parent household, and she is adamant that she lived as a middle-class then upper middle-class individual, never knowing what it meant to be poor. Unfortunately, however, she knows what it means to be hungry, and as a twelve-year-old with low self-esteem, she found herself in a very similar predicament as the poor, hungry protagonists in the novels of Walker and Sapphire: victimized with no knowledge of sex/sexuality, no known allies, and no clear path toward healing and freedom.

Gay's memoir, on the whole, is just as candid as reviewers promise, but she is clearly hesitant in sharing her story, so much so that she spends the first forty pages talking in circles around the incident that changed her life forever. After enduring many pages of circumlocution, a strategy Gay uses to overcome the fear of intensifying her own vulnerability, readers finally learn the nature of sexual assault inflicted on the author. Like that of Celie and Precious, Gay's body and innocence are compromised by someone she trusts.

Gay depicts the horrifying experience of being gang-raped in the woods while taking a bike ride with her first boyfriend and insists that he was "a boy [she] thought [she] loved." Even more, she suggests, "As a sheltered, *good* Catholic girl, I barely understood what was happening," especially since Christopher "was a good boy from a good family living in a good neighborhood" (41, 43, 246). Naively, Gay, as do majority members of society, saw her rapist's membership in a wealthy and well-educated family as a sign of his own respectability, a sign that he was a *good* boy, someone who could be trusted. Unfortunately, there is a clear misconception that only the uneducated and destitute resort to acts of abuse and violence. Just as Christopher's family wealth and status do not prevent him from developing narcissistic and abusive character traits, Gay's wealth and formal education do not protect her from his victimization. Even more, the trauma she endures after the rape is intensified by the fact that the loving, *respectable* people in her home do not notice the change and, therefore, do not come to her aid. And, instead of awareness and safety, a traditional education and respectability politics only offered Gay naïveté and false hopes.

Although not illiterate like Celie and Precious, Gay maintains that she was "smart but not smart," insisting that she "mostly learned about sex from [Judy Blume's] novel *Forever*" (289, 35). In hindsight, she realizes that all of the education she received at schools like Exeter and Yale were not enough to make her "smart," and continually throughout the text, she differentiates between intellect and emotion, proving the point that one's success in a traditional educational setting is insignificant if not accompanied by knowledge of society, sexuality, and self. In other words, she was not smart if her education was one dimensional. Gay might have been "smarter" on the topic of sex and sexuality if she had read books by authors other than Blume (Walker perhaps), if more women would have unapologetically shared their experiences on the often-taboo topic, if respectability politics had not taken her one ally, her mother—the person from whom she claims to have inherited her strength and demeanor.

Reflecting on her mental state after the rape, Gay acknowledges that she was in a perpetual state of loneliness and that playacts of respectability were tiring and damaging. She insists, "At home I tried to be the good girl my parents thought me to be, but it was exhausting. On so many occasions, I wanted to tell them something was wrong, that I was dying inside, but I couldn't find the words. I couldn't find a way to overcome my fear of what they might say or do and think of me" (46). Because she was dying inside, Gay became determined to fill her insides with the pleasure she thought she might never feel again on the outside, the same pleasures that Celie and Precious contrived when they were ashamed of and unfamiliar with the pleasures of their bodies. She became addicted to food.

Gay admits that she gained over thirty pounds in two and a half months because food offered her "the only true pleasure" she knew in high school. She also divulges to readers that while this is not her current weight, at her heaviest, she weighed 577 pounds. And though she clairvoyantly outlines how living in an "unruly" body informs her feminism, what she makes most evident in this memoir is the fact that she "wish[es she] had known that [she] could talk to [her] parents and get help, and turn to something other than food." "I wish," she declares, "I had known that my violation was not my fault" (15). With no representation of what it meant to be self-identified and self-sexualized and a belief, therefore, that she had no one to talk to about her trauma, she engulfed her body with food. In other words, her need for an outlet was not fulfilled, so she took in more toxins in hopes of covering up the things that so desperately needed to come out.

In addition to food, Gay confesses that she had an unconscious desire for sexual pleasure evoked by a man but was afraid of being abused and victimized again and turned to women instead. Denying herself the touch of a man becomes a wall of protection as well as a form of self-inflicted discomfort for Gay. She acknowledges, "For quite some time, I touched but wouldn't allow myself to be touched. I was stone *and* untouchable. I seethed. I was swollen with desire, with a desperate need to be touched, to feel a woman's skin against my skin, to find release through pleasure. I withheld even that from myself. I punished myself" (239). Interestingly enough, even though Gay admits to no longer believing in God after being raped, some ten or twenty years later, she still believes in the waywardness of an explicit and unapologetic sexuality and therefore "punishes" herself for her continued inability to fit prescribed standards and molds. Essentially, while the initial abuse was the fault of Christopher and his friends, the continued abuse and punishment seem to come at the hands of a society that promotes such daunting standards as the politics of respectability.

Luckily, Gay notes that the older she gets, the less she cares about what other people think. Still, she has to check herself every now and again, insisting, "I try to be on the lookout for patterns of behavior, choices I'm making where I'm trying too hard, giving too much, reaching too intently for being right where right is what someone else wants me to be" (255). While this revelation is indeed a positive one, what is most alarming is the fact that she did not begin learning this lesson until her thirties and forties, although her trauma began at age twelve. It is disheartening to think that girls like her live with shame and guilt and suffer in silence for twenty-plus years because sex remains a taboo topic. Of course, strides are being made in today's era with the rise of social media and movements such as #MeToo, but as Gay discovered, breaking the silence is only half the battle, as it is immensely important for one to have support from and be in community with self-identified, self-sexualized, and self-actualized individuals.

In one of the final passages of her memoir, Roxane Gay recalls sitting at a table with her mother after one of her scholarly articles was published. In a very indirect way, her mother gives Gay permission to exhale; she implies that she has been following her daughter's work, that she is aware of her trauma, and that she is sorrowful and not judgmental. Gay states, "My mom had poked at me, in her way, and we had a conversation about how sometimes children, even ones with great parents, are too scared to talk to their parents about trauma they experience . . . We talked about how we hoped the world would be better to my niece, and that if anything happened to her, she would talk to someone" (286). I share Gay's sentiments and, likewise, hope that speaking up will become the new first option for anyone who is victimized. But I also hope that they find a supportive, self-actualized individual on the receiving end of their words. Gay acknowledges that even decades after the rape, her mother, although intentional and supportive, danced around this touchy subject. So, it is clearly not just children who are *too scared* to have these conversations. The more we talk, however, the fewer people will suffer in silence.

Like most practical feminists, Gay admits that she is still in process and that being in community with other radical women is essential to her healing. She states, "I don't know if I am happy, but I can see and feel that happiness is well within my reach. I am not the same scared girl that I was. I have let the right ones in. I have found my voice" (302–3). Even further, she insists, "I am using my voice, not just for myself but for people whose lives demand being seen and heard . . . Writing this book is the most difficult thing I've ever done . . . but I wrote this book because it felt necessary" (303). This is the essence of maverick feminism, first becoming self-identified, self-sexualized, and self-actualized, then using one's own experiences to uplift other Black girls and women and, ultimately, providing them with the tools and support they need in order to uplift themselves and others. Our lives would be much richer (i.e., freer, safer, and more pleasurable) if this were a custom we practiced as opposed to respectability politics, where a shaming seems to ensue instead.

CONCLUSION

In "'Handing Back Shame': Incest and Sexual Confession in Sapphire's *PUSH*" (2005), Elizabeth Donaldson states, "In a certain sense, *PUSH* is a realist, urban version of the romantic, pastoral *Color Purple*" (53). Sapphire herself places her work in conversation with *The Color Purple*, *The Bluest Eye*, and *I Know Why the Caged Bird Sings*. While many have focused on the commonality of sexual abuse displayed in each of these works, the pleasure that Celie and Precious desire and receive after being in community with self-identified, self-sexualized, and self-actualized women is not prominent in critical discussion. Similarly, the connections between food and sexual pleasures in the novels seem to have been overlooked. However, these pleasures, ranging from physical to mental and emotional, counter the abuse inflicted by the men in the protagonists' lives and have a positive impact on their self-worth. Hence, centering these realities, the positive progressions from victims to victors, is a primary focus of this chapter.

On the whole, the narratives analyzed in this chapter, *The Color Purple*, *PUSH*, and *Hunger*, are a noteworthy trifecta representing the limitations of and damages caused to a person who does not receive both a traditional and a sensual education, as proper study in both the book and the body allow women to envision (and hopefully live in) a less violent world with more awareness and stronger alliances. Unfortunately, when Steven Spielberg and Lee Daniels reduced the roles of Shug and Rita in Celie's and Precious's lives respectively, they eradicated a necessary link to healing and wholeness.

I urge that we be more like Walker and Sapphire, and less like Spielberg and Daniels, so that we do not perpetuate over two centuries of abuse and victimization by subscribing to and forcing others to subscribe to respectability politics. Gay's memoir is a testament to the devastation others may cause a victim as well as the havoc one may wreak on self when respectability takes away potential ties to restoration. Do we really want to take blame for someone else experiencing twenty-plus years of isolation and pain on top of the trauma they have already experienced and are too afraid to speak up about? This is the question that I will answer in the next chapter, as I focus more intently on how sisterhoods and intergenerational relationships benefit all involved.

GET IN FORMATION

Sisterhood and the Intergenerational Dynamic

Unlike my father, my mother wasn't comfortable with physical shows of affection. She didn't hug us or kiss us or touch us when she talked to us like he did. Sometimes I think that my mother felt that if she relaxed even a tiny bit, the world she'd so laboriously built to sustain us would fall apart.
—JESMYN WARD, *MEN WE REAPED* (2013)

The critical fixation on Ciara's sheer dress for the 2023 Vanity Fair Oscar Party is indication that sex and sexuality (especially when performed and exhibited by Black women) are still sensitive topics; however, times and attitudes are slowly beginning to shift in a more positive direction concerning popular culture, as popular culture is increasingly being taken a bit more seriously by mainstream society. For instance, Black feminists in academia have taught courses and collaborated to develop syllabi dedicated to Hip Hop and R&B albums such as Beyoncé's *Lemonade* (2016) and Solange's *A Seat at the Table* (2016). Even more, in 2018, rapper Kendrick Lamar won the Pulitzer Prize for music. With his album *DAMN.* (2017), he became the first nonclassical or jazz musician to win this coveted award. His name is now being discussed alongside great poets such as Gwendolyn Brooks, and rightfully so, as his talent, ingenuity, and skill are undeniable in this unapologetically Black, boisterous, and very political album.

In a similar vein, *Red Table Talk*, a web television talk show starring Jada Pinkett Smith and her daughter, Willow Smith, and mother, Adrienne Banfield-Norris, won NAACP Image Awards in 2019 and 2021 and has been nominated for several other awards since its production in 2018, including several nominations for both an Emmy Award and a People's Choice Award. What is most fascinating about this Facebook Watch series is that three generations of women (often in conjunction with celebrity guests) ruminate over and weigh in on topics including motherhood, mental health, sex, gender, fitness, abuse, rape, polyamory, white privilege, pornography, narcissism, addiction, and divorce, all with few to no holds barred. While each of the three women is rather progressive, it is without question that the youngest of the trio, Willow, is the most liberal, and the elder is the most traditional, but all are conscious and receptive of change, particularly when it means improving the lives of self and others. Such is also the case for the characters in Terry McMillan's *Getting to Happy* (2010).

Now over a decade old, and perhaps not thought to have the same level of rigor and depth as the other texts analyzed in this book, McMillan's novel is a prime example of the benefits one gains from willingly engaging in sisterhoods and intergenerational relationships. Four women—Savannah, Robin, Bernadine, and Gloria—from the novel *Waiting to Exhale* (1992) are revisited fifteen years later in this sequel. At or nearing fifty years of age, they have different dilemmas from the women introduced to readers in the previous text but are plagued with disagreeable life circumstances nonetheless. However, while Savannah, Robin, Bernadine, and Gloria, along with their respective problems, joys, and successes, are seemingly the focal point of the narrative, it is, in fact, their offspring (or other relatives) who solidify and help to fulfill the narrative's purpose, which is to promote acceptance, change, sisterhood, and an outright dismissal of respectability politics.

Due to significant generational divides, in order for the four protagonists to have healthy relationships with their children, grandchildren, younger siblings, and nieces and nephews, a meeting of the minds on middle ground is required. This middle ground is the central focus of this chapter, as the following analyses exemplify and reiterate the importance of sisterhoods and intergenerational relationships by examining the relationships between the three generations of women in *Getting to Happy* and illuminating the magnitude to which each of their identities and sexualities are realized and strengthened as a result of the interactions. I argue, consequently, that all four protagonists evolve as more complex individuals, possessing tools to become maverick feminists who are self-identified, self-sexualized, and self-actualized, capable of propelling themselves and others toward freedom and happiness.

In the final section of this chapter, like the final sections of the previous two chapters, I analyze a nonfiction text, Michelle Obama's *Becoming* (2018) in this case, to demonstrate how literature and life intersect, and I reiterate the notion that Black women writers often use literature to affirm and improve the lived experiences of other Black women. In *Eloquent Rage*, Brittney Cooper suggests that respectability politics died when the former First Lady wore a bun to Trump's inauguration in 2017 (147). Indeed, by the end of President Barack Obama's second term in office, Michelle seemed over the shenanigans of presenting herself as respectful and pious only to be endlessly ridiculed by the media and self-righteous onlookers, and standing with her husband to transfer the powers of the highest office of the country to a racist, sexist bigot with little respect for the nation he was elected to lead appeared to be the last straw. However, as I demonstrate through a close, analytical reading of her first memoir, for Michelle Obama (née Robinson), the death of respectability politics was a slow and long-awaited one, as respectability continually waxed and waned in importance in her life, due in part to her parents' intentionality in making sure that she (and her brother) had a relaxed and freeing, yet very connected and supported, upbringing in conjunction with close alliances with Black women who were, likewise, free, unapologetic, vocal, passionate, and, most importantly, happy. Freedom and happiness are what the former First Lady permits herself to experience on that memorable inauguration day in 2017, what she grants her daughters, and what she wishes for all Black women. Readers will see that her narrative is a nonfictional account avowing the effectiveness of the sisterhoods and intergenerational relationships presented in McMillan's fictional work. It is a reminder of the sheer importance of developing and owning one's identity and sexuality while using one's story and voice to advocate for self and others. *Becoming*, likewise, is an authentic testament to respectability politics' debilitating effects on one's psyche.

WHEN DAUGHTER KNOWS BEST:
ROBIN AND SPARROW

In the 2007 essay titled "That the Mothers May Soar and the Daughters May Know Their Names: A Retrospective of Black Feminist Literary Criticism," Farah Jasmine Griffin comments on and is dismayed by the fact that there was once a deficiency of recognized and widely studied Black feminist ancestors. She recalls the rigorous process of many critics, particularly during the 1970s and '80s, "locating, teaching, and writing about earlier 'lost' works by African American women" (340). Alice Walker and Toni Cade Bambara, among other feminists, were influential in making certain that Black feminist foremothers—like Zora Neale Hurston—did indeed soar and that their names, writings, and deeds were known by future generations. Similarly, the characters in *Getting to Happy* are focused on this generation building, as the daughters encourage and often assist in their mothers' elevation. Eventually, there is a mutual reverence of names and legacies, as the characters all benefit from this intergenerational approach to nurturing self-identified, self-sexualized, and self-actualized women. Mutual reverence means that each generation of women shows respect and pays homage to one another in an attempt not to diminish or overlook their counterpart's significant contributions to their lives and well-beings. In other words, McMillan's protagonists all learn that age truly ain't nothing but a number; young girls, too, can/do have something to contribute and, likewise, have all the world to gain.

Robin and Sparrow, the mother-daughter duo most involved in one another's affairs, also have the most setbacks, but the process itself enriches the two women and allows for a stronger sense of respect for the counterpart and a deeper love for and understanding of self. For instance, both mother and daughter are quirky, (mostly) free-spirited individuals, and their eccentricities are highlighted throughout the book, particularly when they are referred to as "Robin and a different bird" (415). Sparrow is acutely aware of her unconventionality and, upon recognizing her mother's attempts at conforming to societal expectations such as respectability politics, is determined to get Robin to understand that difference is not at all a bad quality and that honest, open dialogue and reflection are essential to happiness.

Readers get a glimpse of Robin and Sparrow's relationship during their first dialogue, where Sparrow is encouraging her mother to sign up for an online dating site to avoid the possibility of never "getting laid ever again in life." In response, Robin insists that although she and Sparrow are "best friends and talk about most everything[, t]his topic [sex], however, is off-limits" (20). However, because Sparrow is product of a popular culture–influenced generation and exhibits what Brittney Cooper (2012) calls the "politics of disrespectability," or a knowing disregard for and discarding of the long-burdening respectability politics, she purposely ignores her mother's discomfort with the topic and questions, "Mom, did you catch what I just said?" (20). Robin retorts: "My love life and sex life are none of your business" (20). But why isn't it? Why is this one topic off-limits, particularly when the mother-daughter duo discusses nearly everything else?

This conundrum is further magnified by the fact that Robin has shared with Sparrow very little about her father, except for the fact that he was just a "good lay" (31). Robin admits to readers (not to her daughter) that "back in the good old days, [she] was a little loose" (31). I question, and, seemingly, Sparrow does as well: If those days were, in fact, *good*, why is she now depriving herself of goodness? Robin's friends agree that she was a very sensual being. For example, Savannah insists that Robin is a Miss Congeniality type who "worked in an executive capacity at an insurance company but was still on the verge of becoming a slut" (11). As noted during the discussion of Roxane Gay's memoir, slut shaming is but one of many drawbacks of respectability politics, one that can lead an individual down a long road of isolation, trauma, and self-sabotage. On this idea of slut shaming and in response to her short story "Girl," author Jamaica Kincaid (2014) ponders, "If only I had become a slut." She insists that her mother's respectability politics "ruined sex" for her, and in hindsight, concludes that "a slut is a perfectly *enjoyable* way to go through life; you can't have too much slutdom" (emphasis added).

This idea of reneging on one's sexual politics is one that I plan to further analyze in a future work, as it is common for young Black girls to develop negative views on sex(uality), especially outside of the institution of marriage, as a result of the fears handed down by

generations of women who, in their older years, think more freely
and unapologetically about sex(uality). Sparrow, though, described
by Savannah and Gloria as "a cross between a little Oprah and Annie Oakley," is determined, early on, to end the generational trauma
inflicted by proponents of respectability politics.[1] Besides, in discussing her first sexual encounter, she realizes that a lack of open, honest
dialogue about sex(uality) has already done enough damage. Specifically, at the age of fifteen, Sparrow admits—and Robin has already
discerned—that she has had her first sexual experience: "Tried not
to, but it was difficult, almost impossible to say no" (21). Earlier critical conversations on this off-limits topic might have demonstrated
to Sparrow that she had both the power and agency to say no, that
pressure from high-strung high school boys should not have been
stronger than her will and desire for self-preservation. Luckily, unlike that of Celie and Precious in the novels of Walker and Sapphire
respectively, it does not appear that Sparrow's first sexual encounter
was a violent one, but it was not an empowering experience either.

Sparrow's first sexual encounter is with a guy, Gustav, who is unsure
of his sexual orientation; he confesses to her after they have had sex
that "he *thinks* he's gay." Perhaps he used his experience with Sparrow as a test. However, because sex tends to be equal parts physical,
mental, and spiritual and can, therefore, lead to a transfer of energies
and behaviors, it is not implausible to assume that the negative entity
of uncertainty is transferred to Sparrow when she later declares to
her mother that she "*think*[s her] heart was broken" (303; emphasis
added). Medical doctor Lawrence Wilson (2011) refers to this transfer
of energy as energy attachment and insists, "This is a powerful reason
to not engage in casual sex, even if you are single and unattached. It
is very easy for entities to attach during and after sexual intercourse.
For one thing, the person is vulnerable. For another, ordinary sex
always depletes the body to a degree, and this greatly favors entity
attachment." Essentially, this theory confirms that it is not unusual for
individuals—particularly women because "some entities love being
inside a woman's vagina"—to retain the feelings and energies of their
sexual partners (Wilson). I argue that the ambiguities of Sparrow's
and Gustav's sexual and intimate feelings are not simply due to age,
immaturity, and energy attachment. They are due, likewise, to a lack

of self-sexualization and self-actualization, traits that are developed and enriched when in open conversation and community with people who have already "gone there to know there," a lack that, as demonstrated in the analyses conducted in the previous two chapters, could lead to further risky and detrimental behaviors.

Though not fully evolved, Sparrow clearly has some positive qualities, and perhaps knowing the consequences of not being self-sexualized and self-actualized, Robin is thankful that in most regards, her daughter "has a mind of her own" (22). Mostly she is pleased that Sparrow does not use drugs and attempts to avoid consequences by being "smart about" sex and using contraception (21). Still, Robin is not always willing to try to understand or support Sparrow's thought process, and she is hardly willing to consider just how smart her daughter might be. Robin insists in secret, "She's the daughter. I'm the mother. What makes her think her opinions or her little teenage insights are worth their weight in gold? I know she means well. And there's a small chance she may be right. But you shouldn't let your kids know they know more than you do" (24–25).

Like scholars and school officials who are opposed to engaging texts that unapologetically grapple with the off-limits topic of sex, Robin sees herself in a power struggle, afraid that if she engages ideas proposed by someone traditionally thought less erudite or sophisticated, then, in turn, she will have to relinquish her authority and command, perhaps even lose the respect of her daughter. Additionally, Robin erroneously thinks that blocking out the topic of sex will eradicate any potential problems and demonstrate who is in charge. Fortunately, Sparrow is cut from a different cloth and completely ignores respectability politics, among other societal standards and expectations. Robin knows this but only inwardly appreciates it. She states, "My daughter has chutzpah and a lot of insight for her age. She also thinks she knows everything. I've told her hundreds of times she can't learn everything there is to know about life from watching *Real World* and *Survivor*" (32). Imagine the confidence and impact Sparrow could have if Robin were to more thoroughly foster this chutzpah and insight, particularly in the areas of sex and sexuality. Because she does not, however, Sparrow insists that she knows nothing about love "except what [she has] seen on TV" (26).

Despite knowing little about love, Sparrow is passionate about developing a personal relationship with her mother, but she is especially relentless in her attempt to get her mother to develop a relationship with herself and to climb down off the pedestal that she has created for herself. In brief, Sparrow is insistent on her mother disregarding societal expectations and having an active and positive sexuality and sex life. Thanks to Sparrow's prodding, Robin will later learn that this simultaneous contempt for systems and desires for personal happiness are precisely the stuff that revolutions and change are made of.

In addition to attempting to convince her mother to try online dating, Sparrow also encourages interracial dating. Robin retorts, "Just because you only like white boys, don't try to get me to follow in your footsteps, sweetie." Sparrow assures her mother, "I don't like them because they're white, Mom. I just like them. A lot of black guys at school aren't attracted to girls like me." "I'm my own person," she proudly confirms; "I don't fit the mold" (27). Sparrow is a practiced violinist and a reality television aficionada; there is no surprise that she does not fit the mold. She is essentially one person living within two worlds, a true blend of high and low culture. It is unfortunate that the world, and her own mother, at times, tries to snuff this beauty out of her.

Confident in her own identity, however, Sparrow is on a mission to get her mother to take back her control. She recognizes that societal perceptions have indeed affected Robin's decisions, and while Robin does not accept Sparrow's views on interracial dating, she does take her advice and tries online dating, mainly because this is something she thinks she can do in secret. Robin has momentarily found herself lacking in confidence and is full of desperation, hoping that exaggerating her personal characteristics on several dating websites will attract someone who is "promising." The only promises she gets are unfulfilled as the only man she is attracted to stands her up for their first date, lies about being single and childless, and attempts to take money from her under the false pretense of self-publishing a book of poetry. After this realization, Robin insists that she is done with online dating.

While it is apparent that Sparrow's modern dating convention was not effective for her mother, due in part to Robin's own lies and lack of "chutzpah," Robin's failure at finding love online is not equivalent to the failure of the intergenerational dynamic. In fact, after reflecting on this experience, Robin is now more confident in who she is as a person and as a woman, and she is more aware of what she wants and is unwilling to accept from a man. Shortly after the failed new-age attempt at dating, Robin meets an old friend, Michael, at a gym and rekindles a relationship with him. Fans of *Waiting to Exhale* will remember that the reason she did not appreciate Michael when they were younger was a superficial one: he was overweight. As a result of self-reflection encouraged through the intergenerational relationship with her daughter, however, Robin's judgement of others is now less shallow and restricted. More importantly, she no longer judges herself according to society's mirror. Therefore, her new reasons for being intrigued by Michael at the age of forty-nine are much more personal than her reasons for not liking him years prior. She insists, "I like who you are. What you stand for. I like that you have integrity. I like what you value, and I like your values. Always have. You respect me. You make me feel smart, even though I am smart. You make me feel good. Like warm pudding . . . It's also nice not to have to apologize for what I'm not" (378).

Like her daughter, Robin finally determines and accepts that what she is not is a person who fits the mold. In fact, as opposed to waiting for Michael to take on the traditional male role and ask for her hand in marriage, she asks him, "Would you like to marry me?" and vows, "Even if you put those forty pounds back on, join a circus, get a job flipping burgers at Micky D's—you ain't going nowhere, boyfriend" (377, 378). Because of Sparrow's seeming meddling and the revelation as a result, Robin has determined that it is not only okay for her to not fit the mold, but the man she loves does not have to fit the mold either (although he does have to be Black). By the end of the novel, Robin portrays identifiably maverick feminist characteristics and consents to the changing times, specifically times that suggest that self-sexualization is a natural prerequisite for personal growth and that avowing to respectability politics can be a debilitating experience that, quite frankly, does not grant an individual, or their future generations, a great deal of happiness.

All in all, sisterhoods and intergenerational relationships are designed to benefit both or all parties involved. Robin, at the end of the narrative, can be found soaring, and Sparrow notices and appreciates her growth. According to Sparrow via Bernadine's stepdaughter,

Taylor, Robin "has finally gotten laid and [is] much nicer . . . she's fallen for this super-nice guy Michael, a real blast from her past, and things have gotten hot and heavy and are picking up more steam than a locomotive around their crib, and . . . they're in Napa Valley . . . but they're not picking any grapes. They're bonding" (390). Now that Robin is *nicer* and their home feels happier and more welcoming, Sparrow has the support she needs to battle some of her own troubles.

In the many attempts to talk to her mother about men and sex, Sparrow grew eager to develop a relationship with her father. She states, "You know what occurred to me? That my very own father lives in the same city as I do, and I'm his daughter and I wouldn't know him if I passed him on the street . . . He's actually a nice person who made some stupid choices and he's paid for them . . . You have to open your heart and learn how to forgive others when they disappoint you, Mom. Haven't you always told me that?" (262–63). While this lesson of forgiveness is one that Robin initially taught her daughter, due to Robin's growing fixation on being appropriate and respectable, Sparrow has to reteach this and many other lessons to her mother.

In the end, however, Robin's newfound happiness and the support she can now provide her daughter are testament that the intergenerational dynamic helps individuals to see the world from a newer, freer, more diverse viewpoint. It also attributes to both individual and communal growth. To reiterate, the hope for this type of freedom, acceptance, and growth is the primary reason many Black women authors painstakingly share their narratives, fictional or true. And as Robin and Sparrow's relationship demonstrates, mothers should likewise share with their daughters (and their sons, for that matter). The sharing does not tear down the worlds that were "so laboriously built to sustain [them]," rather it provides the daughters with the information and skill to sustain themselves (Ward 158).

A MOTHER TO THE MOTHERLESS: BERNADINE AND TAYLOR

Next to Robin and Sparrow, the mother-daughter duo that garners significant reader's attention in *Getting to Happy* is Bernadine and

Taylor. Actually, Taylor is not Bernadine's natural daughter; she is the daughter of her first ex-husband and his second wife, Kathleen, the white office assistant for whom John left Bernadine. Though Bernadine has a biological daughter with John, Onika, the majority of her presence in the novel involves accidently coming out to her mother and figuring out the best way to tell her father. There are a few powerful moments between the two, specifically when Bernadine accepts her daughter on her own terms and when they have a heart-to-heart after Bernadine has returned from rehab, but the book does not indicate that Bernadine and Onika's relationship results in any personal growth for Bernadine herself. Taylor, on the other hand, holds a mirror to Bernadine, forces her to reflect on her choices and actions (or the lack thereof), causes her to become uncomfortable, but also assures her that she has the support needed to change and grow.

When Bernadine is introduced in this sequel, she is divorced for a second time and addicted to prescription drugs such as Xanax, Ambien, and Zoloft. Bernadine's medical dependency is a result of depression caused by the second divorce. She finds out, via his first wife, that her second husband, James, is going by an alias and has a second family, does not work in the career he professes, and has pilfered a large amount of her money over time. Needless to say, Bernadine is in desperate need of some happiness.

Furthermore, when readers meet Taylor, she is fourteen years old and distraught by the fact that her mother has left her and her father and gone to London with another man. As a result, Bernadine is the only mother figure she has. However, because Bernadine is dependent on drugs and not often in control of her own life, she can do little to assist Taylor during her personal trauma. Thus, like Sparrow does for Robin, Taylor steps in to help build Bernadine back up so that Bernadine can, in turn, be the positive mother figure she needs in her life. In both cases, the mother soars because the daughter desperately needs her to.

Taylor affectionately refers to Bernadine as "MomMom," indicating that she is a second mother to her. Although in pleading with her second mother to take her first mother's place and take her in, Taylor expresses to Bernadine, "You've been more of a mom to me than she has" (166). Bernadine denies this assertion. Still, Taylor insists, "I can't live with my dad, MomMom. I just can't. Things are so screwed up in our house. He's never there, and then let's throw in my slutty mom who bails on her own kid just so she can get screwed by some British guy" (165). Taylor, like Sparrow, is looking for peace, happiness, and support in her home; she, likewise, does not shy away from seemingly off-limits topics. To some, Taylor's reference to her mother as "slutty" may seem inappropriate and disrespectful. However, in her eyes, she is justified in using this language. John has already revealed to Bernadine that Kathleen had "been fooling around for a while [and] made [Taylor] swear to secrecy" (121). These actions, to a teen living in a society where women with deviant or unapologetic sexualities are intrinsically demeaned and shunned, are equivalent to sluttiness; in addition, she cannot seem to fathom any reason other than "slut-like" (read sexual) practices as the reason why her mother would even consider "bailing" on her and her father.

Despite her feelings about her mother, Taylor recognizes the importance of having healthy allies and being involved in a positive intergenerational relationship. Therefore, she pleads with Bernadine, "Even though I'm a teenager, I'm still a child and I don't want to grow up and become a totally twisted grown-up just because I was deprived of some basic shit they say we need as children—like love and attention. Is that like asking for too much?" (171). Even with Taylor's crass language, the staunchest supporters of respectability politics cannot help but empathize with her: This lack of basic shit is precisely why Janie and Winter endured countless tragedies on their lonesome journeys to invent and find happiness. This lack of basic shit is precisely why Celie and Precious endured violence and sexual abuse for so long. Taylor is not willing to take these risks. She quickly learns that her own survival and growth are dependent on the survival and growth of others and vice versa. In other words, she learns the importance of being in community with self-identified, self-sexualized, and self-actualized women, especially a mother figure.

Taylor recognizes Bernadine's dependency on prescription drugs and offers advice and guidance to Bernadine so that Bernadine can someday offer advice and guidance to her. She insists, "If you're strung out, you should check yourself into a facility" (167). Bernadine denies being "strung out," but Taylor's rebuttal to every single reason

Bernadine suggests she needs her pills forces Bernadine, inwardly, to consider the fact that she might, indeed, be strung out. Taylor maintains that she, too, has trouble sleeping some nights due to worries about certain issues, yet she is adamant that she does not resort to medication each time one of these occurrences takes place.[2] Furthermore, because Bernadine sees Taylor's youth as an indication of a lack of experience and ponders what valid causes for worry or concern she may have about life, Taylor clarifies, "Duh. Just finals and driving, and sex and drugs and boys and why did my mom desert me and my dad, and what do I want to be when I grow up and is there a college out there waiting for me and what box do I check when they ask my race? I could go on" (169). Taylor's concerns range from juvenile to more serious to universal. But unlike Bernadine, she is not attempting to ignore or even face those issues all at once. More specifically, she is not concerned with putting on a front for society, not concerned with appearing perfect. Instead, her concern is having a mother she can look up to, confide in, and gain support from when she has to tackle each of her problems individually. In essence, she is more concerned with progress as opposed to plaudits, which unfortunately are the basis of respectability politics.

Without Bernadine's approval, Taylor begins to spread the word, specifically to her father, that Bernadine is going away "on a trip" to "attend some special cooking course," having full awareness that the fear of telling people she has a problem is a central part of Bernadine's problem (229). Bernadine adheres to and is a victim of both the politics of respectability and the strong Black woman stereotype because the image she presents to others is far more important than her own self-image, and admitting that she misuses drugs and, therefore, lacks control, presumably, makes her both weak and undeserving of respect. In starting this rumor about a cooking course, Taylor attempts to protect her MomMom's image and pride while setting her on the proper path for necessary improvement and growth. Consequently, Bernadine, like Robin in reference to Sparrow's intergenerational involvement, realizes "that Taylor was on to something and that as soon as her head stops spinning, she should make that call" (230).

Ultimately, Sparrow and Taylor have different methods but the same objectives: to have a whole, happy, and self-identified mother, and to have a fulfilling relationship with that mother. Their difference in method can be attributed to their different interests and upbringings. Whereas Sparrow and Robin watch "stupid movies" together, Taylor's father, on the other hand, makes her watch *60 Minutes* and CNN (210). She states, "I hated it at first, but now I feel like I know a lot of important stuff, fascinating stuff, actually. Plus, Anderson Cooper is such a fox—gay or not" (167). Taylor does have knowledge of a great amount of "important stuff"; chief among the important information is the significance and impact of sisterhoods and companionships with self-identified, self-sexualized, and self-actualized women.

Robin hated to admit that Sparrow was knowledgeable for her age; equally so, Bernadine notices how much important stuff Taylor knows and admits that "this girl reminded her so much of Rona Barrett from way, way back, it wasn't funny" (390).[3] This comparison suggests that Taylor possesses recognizably mature and curious characteristics, but she has learned to adapt them in her twenty-first-century, teenage world in a way that benefits others, particularly Bernadine, who admits that she gets a "kick out of" Taylor's mannerisms and language use, her unashamed and self-assured display of disrespectability politics. Taylor's freedom frees Bernadine in a manner that she was not aware existed in that stage of her life, a freedom she was not aware she needed but would soon greatly appreciate.

When Bernadine finally does make "that call" and admits to herself, the receptionist, and her family and friends that she has a problem, she "feels a sense of calmness inside. Xanax has never made her feel this way" (313). Because of Taylor's seeming meddling, Bernadine rejects and throws off the shackles of the politics of respectability and the strong Black woman stereotype. While in rehab, she could not deny, as she previously had to Taylor, that she was strung out, and thanks to Taylor's insistence on Bernadine checking herself into a facility, Bernadine is better able to recognize her own assets, become self-identified, and reject and ignore popular opinion, not for the mere purpose of being oppositional or confrontational, but for the necessity of being free within herself. As a premise of maverick feminism, this personal freedom is a requirement for soaring and for uplifting others.

After Bernadine completes her time in rehab, she has officially gained a new appreciation and respect for Taylor and her difference of perspective. John picks Bernadine up from the facility and relays a message that his "other daughter" would like to speak with her; he uses "other" to indicate the fact that she is not the daughter of whom he and Bernadine share parentage. However, Bernadine quickly corrects him and refers to Taylor as "*our*" daughter (387; emphasis original). Before her rehab and revelation, Bernadine referred to Taylor as one of the "unfortunate mixed-race children who got too many genes from one parent and not enough from the other" (164). Now, she refers to herself as one of Taylor's "other parents."

In the end, Taylor meets her goal of helping to uplift her Mom-Mom so that her MomMom can, in turn, help to uplift her. And like Sparrow does once she feels confident in her mother's happiness and ability to support her, Taylor insists that it is time for her to tackle other problems and foster other relationships. Thus, when Bernadine assures Taylor that everything in rehab "went fine," Taylor replies, "I'm glad to hear it, MomMom. So. The other thing is this. I've been doing some serious thinking, and I have come to the conclusion that it would be better if I stayed with my dad because he's lonely and he's got that big prostate issue, and I think he needs me. Plus, he's been coming home earlier, and we've been talking about all kinds of things. I never knew he was so interesting" (390). This response portrays Taylor as an intelligent young lady very much capable of assisting in the growth of others well beyond her years; it also indicates that she recognizes and appreciates the value of the intergenerational dynamic, or talking about "all kinds of things" and validating the interests of others. When no topic is off-limits, one's knowledge and ability to soar is not limited either. In contrast, respectability and piety place further limitations on the already marginalized, with the probability of soon rendering them illiterate and ineffective.

Overall, like Robin and Sparrow, both Bernadine and Taylor benefit from their relationship. Taylor, as demonstrated above, gains a soaring mother and is in the business of helping her father to soar as well, and both parents recognize that they need her just as much as she needs them. Bernadine, of course, becomes clean again, although not in a virginal or sexual sense because her intimate and sensual interests actually increase after she becomes (newly) self-identified. She jokes with her girlfriends in a bridal shop about virginal brides versus brides who "couldn't wait," and during the final scene of the novel, the women "look like they have seen a ghost" when Bernadine agrees with Robin's viewpoint on sex and admits that she one day hopes to have both a relationship and relations again. She states, "I'm not dead. I've been frozen for a while. As you guys can tell, I'm thawing out" (409, 419). Indeed, self-identification and self-sexualization are interconnected, and her thawing out is equivalent to relinquishing the strongholds of respectability politics that once limited her ability to get to happy. Furthermore, with her happiness in mind, she soon enrolls in culinary school so that she can open the business of her dreams. Most importantly, she recognizes that times have indeed changed, that she does not want to get left behind, and that it is important to know and be confident in her whole self—sexuality, weaknesses, and all—when she finally gets to where she is going.

FROM THE MOUTH OF BABES:
GLORIA AND HER GRANDCHILDREN

In Gayl Jones's *Corregidora* (1975), the protagonist, Ursa Corregidora, grapples between trying to rectify or dismiss a past that has haunted the lives of her mother, grandmother, and great-grandmother before her. The words of Ursa's ex-slave great-grandmother remain poignant in her mind as she attempts to operate and have relationships in the mid- to late twentieth century. Ursa was supposed to produce the next generation, leave evidence of the trauma of slavery and forced miscegenation, "*because they didn't want to leave no evidence of what they done—so it couldn't be held against them*" (14; emphasis original). However, after the actions of Ursa's abusive husband, she undergoes a hysterectomy and determines that she has let down her foremothers, that "there'd be plenty [she] couldn't give back now" (6). As a result, she continues on a path of rememories and regrets, allowing words from generations past to determine her life's path.

Rememory is a theory coined by Toni Morrison. What differentiates the concept of rememory from that of a simple memory is the fact that in a rememory, the character/person remembering the particular event may or may not have physically experienced the event but is psychologically affected by it nonetheless. Lucille P. Fultz recollects a 1989 conversation with Morrison at Princeton—"She suggested that I think of [rememory as] a radio with its volume turned to the lowest point, beyond audibility but never turned off"—and therefore defines rememory as a "remembrance fraught with abhorrent images at times too painful and frightening to face, at other times poignant and memorable" (118, 75). In McMillan's *Getting to Happy*, words between grandmother and grandchildren are equally life altering as Ursa's rememory of her family's past. However, in this case, the wise words are not handed down from the older generation to the younger. Instead, the wise words come from Gloria's toddler and preschool-age granddaughters.

When readers first meet Gloria, she is preparing to celebrate her fourteenth wedding anniversary with Marvin, her loving husband. She is reportedly the only one of the four women who is happily married; this fact quickly changes, however, when Marvin becomes an innocent bystander in a gang shootout on the day of his and Gloria's anniversary. After Marvin's death, Gloria seeks companionship in food, resorts to silence, and has little to no interaction with others until she is forced to care for her grandchildren, who eventually aid in Gloria's growth and continuation on a positive path.

Gloria has four grandchildren, two boys and two girls. The boys, Brass and Stone, are twelve and six years old respectively; the girls, Blaze and Diamond, are four and two. Gloria loves how each of her grandchildren has their own individual personality. Brass is cocky, Stone is smart, Blaze is high-spirited, and Diamond is a "sweet little devil" (63). After mourning Marvin's death for nearly seven months, Gloria admits that her grandchildren brighten her day in a way that no one else does; she looks forward to spending time with them. When her daughter-in-law, Nickida, is incarcerated for mishandling money on her job with the IRS, Gloria gets to spend even more time with her grandchildren, and it is during this time that her own growth takes place.

Gloria picks Blaze and Diamond up from preschool one day, and Blaze and her friends teach Gloria a lesson while she kindly and excitingly participates in playtime with the girls before taking her grandchildren home. She enters the classroom viewing it as "Santa's workshop of little black elves," but she leaves viewing the children, particularly the girls, as substantial human beings, keepers of society, and, for this reason, begins to give them even more nourishment and care (271). Early on, however, she realizes that the children have different views of the world, and they help to change and shape her views as well.

Gloria joins Blaze and four of her preschool classmates in a children's play kitchen as they prepare a meal over a stove, wash dishes in a sink, and handle business on a headset, carrying out what they assume to be traditional female roles. She offers them an additional job and asks if she can get her hair and makeup done. When she offers to pay with a check, one of the young girls boldly states, "No! They don't take no checks only credit cards." Times had clearly changed, and Gloria notes that the girl, who "looks like she's already seen some things," is a bit too certain about her statement, "as if she has had run-ins like this before" (273). People often say that children (and the elderly) have no filter, as they regularly speak what is on their minds, and this quality is often praised and admired by others. Interestingly, due to respectability politics, when these same children become adults, this very fire is often discouraged and extinguished. Luckily, Blaze and her friends are too young to be tainted by the restraints of respectability and are willing to voice their passions and grievances unapologetically.

As a result of the above conversation in the play area, in addition to a few others, upon leaving the group that she now determines is made up of wise children as opposed to little elves, Gloria hugs them and thinks:

All these miniature people are real people. That one day they'll grow up and become real adults and they'll fall in love, and some of them will have their hearts broken and cry and wonder if they'll ever recover. Some of them will probably get married and have babies and their husbands might die when they least expect it. Or one day they'll be grandparents and their adult children will need them again, which is why Gloria is going to take two of these children to her house until their father, her only son, tells her just how long he needs all of them to stay. (274)

During Gloria's time in the play area—the scene depicting an inadvertent intergenerational dynamic—she realizes that it is beyond time to end her own course of self-pity so that she can be strong enough to aid in the uplift of the next generation. Like Taylor does for Bernadine, Blaze and her classmates unwittingly urge Gloria to develop maverick feminist characteristics, to work on her own personal issues so that she can be sound enough to aid in the uplift of the next generation of women, because, as she notes, they, too, will get married, have children, lose husbands, become grandparents, or, like Sparrow and Taylor, lose their mother or have less than fulfilling first-time sexual encounters.

Essentially, the purpose of the intergenerational dynamic is not to make a paradigm so that future generations will have a model to follow, but rather the goal is to elevate both (or all) parties to their highest height by first recognizing, understanding, engaging, appreciating, and supporting one another's differences and resulting propensity to affect change. In a nutshell, it is teamwork and community, facing any obstacle with the reassurance that through the intergenerational dynamic, one has the advantage of youth and experience, ingenuity and authority, wildness and restraint, passion and poise, the advantage of a complex and complete self.

Shortly after the playtime engagement, because she is now more attentive to her grandchildren's words and actions, Gloria recognizes a change in her youngest grandchild, Diamond, and although she is not pleased with all that she hears during this interaction, she is undoubtedly enlightened. Diamond is nearing three years old. She has uttered words previously, but when readers are introduced to her, they learn that her speech and dialogue are minimal; it is assumed that her lack of communication is a result of autism. However, while Gloria is, again, helping out her son by overseeing her grandchildren, Diamond speaks. Her words are not eloquent or poetic in the sense that one would be surprised to hear a two-year-old utter them; she simply says "Thank you" after Gloria presents her with candy. "Can you say that again, sweetheart?" Gloria asks. And, when she does repeat herself, Gloria honors her with "a hug so strong it lifted Diamond high off the ground." The sassy, intelligent Blaze feels compelled to enlighten her grandmother once again: "She can say more than that . . . She just talks when she feels like it" (330). Readers quickly learn that while

Diamond's failure to speak may have been initiated by her disability, she knowingly limits her communication as a form of resistance.

After learning about Nickida's imprisonment, Gloria asks the girls if they miss her presence. Blaze speaks up, and with a viewpoint different from Taylor's in the previous section, suggests that she does not miss her mom "all the time" because she is mean and "hits hard"; Diamond nods her head in agreement. Attempting to salvage her mother's image and appease her grandmother, however, Blaze assures Gloria that her mother has never hit Diamond; she simply "shaked her back and forth" in an attempt to get her to talk (329). Nickida shaking Diamond in an attempt to get her to speak as opposed to seeking professional help to learn why she is not speaking is similar to Bernadine overmedicating herself to avoid her depression. Neither are effective treatments or coping mechanisms, but because respectability is already being used as a coping mechanism (to garner respect amid continued racism, sexism, classism, ableism, etc.) and because African Americans have a history of distrust for authority, self-diagnosing, self-medicating, or ignoring the problem altogether are not uncommon "solutions." Unfortunately, these remedies often result in further trauma and reduced happiness and joy.

It does not take long for Gloria to learn the importance of taking action to affect change and improve the lives of her future generations, however. After several months of harboring a $300,000 insurance check for Marvin's death, she notes that there was no reason to deposit it until she recognized how much her grandchildren needed her and how much she needed them. She begins to understand that her own survival depends on the survival of future generations, and the survival of future generations depends on her own survival and investment in them. Therefore, she gives half of the $300,000 to her son, Tarik, to aid his unexpected status as a single parent, sends a gracious amount to Hurricane Katrina victims, and sets "aside a nice sum to guarantee Oasis was going to be one of the hippest, sexiest, up-to-the-minute state-of-the-art-salon-and-spas in Phoenix." The hipness of her salon includes unique jewelry, "some of which will be made by Ms. Sparrow" (339).

Ultimately, Gloria's investment in the future is a plan to avoid getting caught in the past, a deliberate effort to maintain a dynamic presence in an ever-evolving society. Accepting this change and hoping to be whole, confident, effective, and happy in the midst of it, she works toward becoming self-identified and self-sexualized when she joins Weight Watchers and makes a purchase at Good Vibrations, an adult novelty store. Marvin had previously been the person to prepare healthy meals for her and make sure that she walked the necessary miles to remain healthy and fit; he had also been the sole source of her "good vibrations." Therefore, earlier in the novel when Gloria "felt a tinge of excitement at the thought that you could actually buy the kind of penis you always wanted," she is adamant that she had not been thinking about a penis. "If she had," the narrator assures, "it would've been Marvin's. As things stood, she had accepted the fact that she might never be sexually active again. And it was okay" (187). Was it really okay? Clearly it wasn't, as demonstrated through her later purchase. Instead, she had been trying desperately to adhere to the politics of respectability, to deny her natural sexual desires.

What she learns is that it is ludicrous to assume that desires for pleasure will disappear after fourteen years of passionate sex with a man simply because that man dies. Like Bernadine, who admits that the sensual part of her had been frozen, Gloria's commitment to being respectable causes her to believe that her sexuality has to die when Marvin does, unless she remarries, of course. However, as a result of the interactions with her grandchildren, she, by the end of the novel, recognizes and accepts the significance of being able to do for oneself; pleasing herself sexually is no exception. All in all, Blaze and Diamond help and urge their grandmother, or Gawa as they call her, to soar, and she, thus, continues on a path akin to maverick feminism, evaluating and enrichening self in order to be fit to uplift others.

CUT FROM THE SAME CLOTH:
SAVANNAH AND HER RELATIVES

When readers meet Savannah Jackson, she is on the verge of getting a divorce from her husband, Isaac, a porn addict. Despite Isaac's compulsive sexual desire, unlike her three best friends, Savannah has no offspring with whom to interact directly. She has no children of her own and, therefore, no grandchildren, nor does her ex-husband have any children from previous relationships, no children for whom she might serve as a guiding figure or second mother. However, Savannah is the only one of the four friends who has a somewhat tightknit community of relatives. And these relatives, hundreds of miles away, help Savannah realize the importance of family and relationships, despite their differences of opinion and way of living.

Terry McMillan's Savannah Jackson is akin to Toni Morrison's (1973) Sula Peace in the sense that they both come from lower socio-economic backgrounds and have deep ties to their place of birth, although they no longer allow themselves to fit in or connect with that place. Because of their adventurous and calculating characteristics, they leave home and experience life in a fuller, less-restricted manner. Both Savannah and Sula question their upbringings, specifically the fact that their mothers do not represent an image of wedded virtue. However, while readers are allowed to see Sula make a physical re-turn to her hometown of Medallion, Ohio, Savannah's return to Pitts-burgh, Pennsylvania, is only figurative, via phone interactions with her mother and sister. Yet like Sula, Savannah learns that she is indeed her mother's daughter and that the people and community she fled from, ultimately, are what keep her connected to life in other places.

Although Savannah is the last protagonist analyzed in this study, she is the first of McMillan's four characters to introduce herself to readers.[4] She is turning down an invitation to go on a business trip with Isaac, insisting that she is not the type of wife who simply wants to "sit around the pool all day reading romance novels . . . [or] sip on margaritas and eat nachos, or linger in the malls for hours with their husbands' credit cards, trying on resort wear for the cruise they're all going on in the near future." "I'm not crazy about cruises," she insists; "I went on one with Mama and my sister, Sheila, and those long narrow hallways give me the creeps . . . by day four I was ready to jump off our balcony and backstroke home" (2). This passage in the opening pages of the novel reveals Savannah's character. While it suggests that she is independent and is not the stereotypical wife who relies on her husband's income or presence for fulfillment, it also implies that she does not adhere to the same respectability politics that many Black and/or Christian women abide by, as being obedient or submissive to her husband is not one of her top priorities. On the contrary, however, she does permit these same politics to coerce her into the marriage in the first place, admitting that she married Isaac because that seemed to be what was expected of "a forty-year-old love starved black woman who'd never been married" (5). Savannah straddles the fence of respectability continuously throughout the narrative, submitting and not submitting, but her family gives her the wakeup call that she needs in order to finally get to happy.

Savannah has a strong need for agency and control over her circumstances and surroundings. This desire to determine her own surroundings is precisely why she visits Pittsburgh as little as possible. Still, she has a very intriguing relationship with her mother and sister, and after she informs them of her imminent divorce, their relationships seem to become even more vital. These relational developments are important because her relatives remind her of who she is (and is not) as well as who they are (and are not). As a result of the mirrorlike images presented and oftentimes forced on her by her mother and sister, Savannah becomes a more self-identified and self-actualized individual. Thus, her divorce becomes more about reconciling with the past and reviving herself and less about punishing Isaac for his "sinful" ways.

It has been established that Savannah is a woman who likes control; the fact that she does not have offspring is a result of her choosing to control her own body. She chose to have a tubal litigation and, therefore, cannot have children. Her sister sees this as an act of selfishness because "the only person [Savannah] has to worry about is Savannah" (199). However, Savannah's professional interests indicate that she is, indeed, concerned with more people than herself. The work that she does with the television program is geared toward depicting tragic events and circumstances of African American communities in hopes of changing perceptions and opinions about how African Americans do and should live life. She insists that "producing television shows about cultural and social issues" is just as interesting and important as anything anyone else could do to beautify or enhance humanity (2). I am confident that McMillan, and many other Black women authors, particularly those discussed in this study, would make this same argument about their writings, that they are a form of advocacy and protest intended to beautify and enhance humanity.

Interestingly, Savannah prides herself on depicting accurate images of both "good and bad" in Black communities, despite the fact that she is not accepting of the images of good and bad depicted in her own family. She is slightly repulsed by and sarcastically ignores her sister when Sheila suggests that she do a television show about the teen girls in Pittsburgh who "act like they never heard of birth control." Sheila insists that "they get excited about being pregnant. A diploma is not their ticket to financial freedom. A baby is income" (199). This reality seems to be literally too close to home for Savannah, especially since her own sister, although not a teenager or single mother, struggles significantly with her husband to provide for their six children, none of whom Savannah has an active relationship with as an aunt. In fact, Sheila is adamant that Savannah does not "even know [her] kids' names" (199). Savannah seems to use this self-isolation from her nieces and nephews as a way to avoid confronting the similarities between her family and the people that she documents in her shows. She cannot make, and is not allowed to make, this separation from her sister, however, because she has known and loved her all of her life. Ultimately, Shelia's presence in Savannah's life debunks Savannah's desultory façade of respectability.

Savannah admits, although to readers and not to her sister, "The thought of Sheila coming out here made my heart race. I think I'd take GoGo—whoever he is—over her, which is pretty sad to admit" (203). GoGo is Savannah's nephew, Sheila's sixteen-year-old son, who has been expelled from school for using illegal drugs. Sheila thinks that it would help his attitude and keep him out of trouble if he spends a few weeks at Savannah's house in Phoenix. Savannah confesses that her sister is "one of the main reasons I've sent Mama tickets to come out here to visit instead of going back there so much. The way Sheila's been struggling for the past twenty-odd years breaks my heart. She has settled for so little, it's like she never had dreams." This idea of never having dreams is reminiscent of Gwendolyn Brooks's poem "kitchenette building," where the author insists that "'Dream' makes a giddy sound, not strong / Like 'rent,' 'feeding a wife,' 'satisfying a man.'" Sheila has already acknowledged the differences between Savannah's dreams and her own realities; Savannah is still in process.

Readers gather that the true reason Savannah wants to avoid her sister is because she is aware that they are "a lot alike when it gets right down to it." She insists, "We are our mother's daughters" (203). Indeed, the practice of respectability politics has never erased history. After all, Henry Louis Gates Jr. was arrested for "breaking into" his own home in 2009 when a 911 caller reported a suspicious man entering a residence in the Cambridge, Massachusetts, neighborhood. In this case, suspicious was synonymous with Black. Candice Jenkins explores this concept in her work *Black Bourgeois: Class and Sex in the Flesh* and suggests that "material privilege [does not] offer any real protection from the operation of black vulnerability" (7). In other words, due to centuries of systemic and individual racism, the Black body, even in hard-earned, middle-class spaces, is always vulnerable and, seemingly, out of place. Gates was already aware, and Savannah will soon learn, too, that a physical separation from the Black community is possible, but a metaphysical separation is not. Essentially, her efforts to improve the lives of poverty-stricken African Americans are also a step toward improving her own life. Accepting these truths and the many similarities between her and her sister are what will allow them to forge a stronger bond, a bond that can make each sister more powerful and better equipped to take on their individual worlds. This is the essence of sisterhood, the essence of community, the essence of maverick feminism.

For Savannah, it is one thing to be from the ghetto but an entirely different thing to be still in the ghetto. As previously indicated, she likes the idea of doing work that improves humanity, but she does not like having to admit that her family is part of the population that society often thinks needs improving; they taint her image of respectability. When she learns that she has diabetes, though, and the doctor questions the medical history of her parents, the fact that she is her mother's daughter takes on an entirely different meaning. She can speak to the medical history of her maternal family but can only utter in a seemingly nonchalant manner that she has never met her father. It is in this instance that Savannah begins to appreciate her mother and sister more. She recollects a conversation with her sister, a moment when Sheila insists, "You don't exactly break your neck to come to

Pittsburgh—where you were born and raised in case you forgot. The only time we see you is when somebody dies or you just feel guilty" (198). Undeniably, Savannah does feel guilty. In fact, she had made initial plans to go to Paris to reconcile with her diabetes diagnosis, but her mother, like Sheila, insists, "Hell, Pittsburgh is foreign to you. It ain't exactly no postcard but you ain't been here in years." And like Bernadine admitting that she is a drug addict, Savannah exhales and replies, "I would like to come home for Christmas if that's all right with you" (368). This is her first step toward relinquishing the strongholds of respectability politics by rejecting the salvific wish and her first step toward a stronger sisterhood and intergenerational relationship. This is also her first step toward self-fulfillment and personal improvement and her first step toward having a greater impact on the community.

In the end, Savannah has to be rousted by her mother and sister and diagnosed with an illness before she completely breaks free from the shackles of respectability politics, before she accepts the fact that there is "good and bad" in her own family. Furthermore, she consents that while her mother and sister do not have the education or status that she does, they do have a clearer understanding of the social injustices she is concerned with. Their consistent disapproval of how she presents cultural and social issues encourages her to change her television show format, from more of a documentary layout to a "talk show" format, in order to keep up with the times and really reach the people she theorizes about (418).

Like the aforementioned protagonists, Savannah gains a great deal from her interactions with her family; the most important lesson her sister and mother teach her is one that many contemporary feminists/activists have begun to live by: in order to teach the people, one has to be able to reach the people (family included). Hoping to have an effective and long-lasting reach, in addition to changing her show format, Savannah begins eating healthier to counteract her diabetes, and most importantly, she "remember[s] who [she is]. And what [she's] going to do about it" (255). She is the daughter of a single mother, the sister of a low-income woman in an unstable relationship, the ex-wife of a porn addict, and the aunt of a drug abuser. Still, she is Savannah

Jackson, a wealthy and successful Black woman whose main goal is to "paint portraits of our lives, good or bad [because] we need to be able to see how we behave instead of ignoring it" (101). This lesson was made plain to her through the sisterhood and intergenerational relationships with her sister and mother respectively (101).

Fundamentally, Terry McMillan's *Getting to Happy* serves as an example of how happy mediums can be reached, particularly between multiple generations, when respectability politics is no longer a guiding principle. As the protagonists in the novel learn, each individual is just as important to the community as the community is to the individual. Furthermore, forceful attempts at prescribed notions do not guarantee favorable or expected results. And cutting down one's own community only leaves the population vulnerable for others to come in and cause continued ruination.

Overall, this novel is one of the few African American texts in which the Black daughter is not the obvious protagonist but has a clear and essential voice. The features that seemingly banish the daughters to the margins—age and controversial beliefs—are precisely the features that make room for them. As illustrated, the success of sisterhoods and intergenerational relationships are not based on one individual getting "hip" and conforming to the belief system of the other; mutual respect and recognition are important, even between mothers and daughters. After all, a world in which each generation lacks individuality and simply carries out the practices and beliefs of the one that precedes it would seem to evoke perpetual dismay and dullness. It would be a world where Harriet Tubman would not have dared to free slaves, a world where Claudette Colvin would not have dared to remain in her seat, a world where Bree Newsome would not have dared to climb that flagpole, and a world where Michelle Obama would not have dared to hug Queen Elizabeth. I don't know about you, but I don't want to live in that hidebound, orthodox world. I also won't ask other Black women to live in it and give up what, for centuries, has made us unique, memorable, powerful, feared, and heard. I especially won't ask them to give up these attributes to appease the sensibilities of a patriarchal society that would rather not see or hear us at all.

A WIND THAT THREATENED TO UNSETTLE
EVERYTHING: MAVERICK FEMINISM AND OUR
FOREVER FIRST LADY, MICHELLE OBAMA

In her memoir *Becoming* (2018), Michelle Obama shares that her parents always treated her and her brother like autonomous beings, and she discusses the major role music and popular culture played in her life due to close relationships with her grandfather, older cousins, and other relatives; she also relays details about and relationships with many individuals who were self-identified, unapologetic, and advocatory. One of such people who influenced her early on in her life later became her husband and the first African American president of the United States, but the others were mostly women, women who had experienced life (or were experiencing it at that moment) and thought it wise to share their lessons and/or joys with Michelle. These key factors in her life, I argue, are precisely why Michelle Obama felt confident in embracing the queen and why she views her sexuality as a strength as opposed to an inappropriate weakness.

There is no secret that Mrs. Obama is not the only member of a First Family to break royal protocol with Queen Elizabeth II. In fact, former president Donald Trump broke protocol on several different occasions and with multiple offenses, including shaking hands with, walking in front of, and reportedly being late for an engagement with the queen. Does this make him a maverick feminist? Of course not. (If we were on the streets, my response would be "hell nawl!") Then, why are Michelle's actions more justifiable than his? Easy. Trump is no stranger to breaking tradition and thinking that he is above laws and rules. His "alleged" infractions are varied in degrees of horrendousness, including but not limited to sexual assault, tax and insurance fraud, obstruction of justice, bribery, conspiracy to defraud the United States, campaign finance violations, and inciting riots and violence. He is the only US president to be impeached twice, with one of those charges being abuse of power. Donald Trump is the poster boy for toxic masculinity and heteropatriarchal white supremacy. Therefore, he is the antithesis of maverick feminism.

The former First Lady, on the other hand, notes that her seeming disregard for protocol was spurred by a moment of intimacy and compassion, a moment of sisterhood, and a recognition of how the most minute representations of respectability politics and patriarchy (women in dresses and heels) can be damaging even to women of the highest standing. I am aware that there are Black feminist scholars who argued that Queen Elizabeth II protected and preserved heteropatriarchal white supremacy through empire and neocolonial practices, and the recent claims by Prince Harry and Duchess Meghan seem to support this argument. However, the former First Lady suggests that, for just a moment, she blocked out any possible ways Queen Elizabeth II may have supported racial oppression and homed in on one very visible way that she, as a woman, was oppressed by patriarchy. In discussing this first visit to Buckingham Palace, Michelle insists, "Forget that she [Queen Elizabeth II] sometimes wore a diamond crown and that I'd flown to London on the presidential jet; we were just two tired ladies oppressed by our shoes. I then did what's instinctive to me anytime I feel connected to a new person, which is to express my feelings outwardly. I laid a hand affectionately across her shoulder" (318). First Lady Obama's ability to forget systems, to make personal connections with other women, and to express her feelings outwardly are a result of an unrestricted upbringing, an audaciousness gained from being a child of the mainstream, and a spirit fostered by women who were likewise passionate and progressive. She hugged the queen because she had maverick feminist characteristics, and her memoir, like McMillan's *Getting to Happy*, is a testament to the benefits of being a participant in and contributor to sisterhoods and intergenerational dynamics; it is also a testament to the benefits of becoming self-identified, self-sexualized, and self-actualized, or, simply, as her memoir is so aptly titled, *becoming*.

Many adults will admit that they have similar characteristics, mannerisms, and goals as the people who nurtured them. Women might wear the same brand underwear and use the same brand deodorant as their mothers. Men might wear the same brand cologne and use the same brand aftershave as their fathers. Because parents know the magnitude of influence their choices and actions have on their children, many try to present their own lives as pristine, hoping that their children will become "good and wholesome" adults. These parents often require their children to uphold the standards of the politics of respectability when, in fact, they did not or do not adhere to the rules themselves (again, more on this of "reneging" in a future work). They assume that being "good and wholesome" will grant their children a certain degree of acceptance in American society and will allow them to achieve and accomplish as much as or more than they did. This, fortunately, was not Michelle Obama's childhood.

The former First Lady admits that she treasured adults' reactions when she told them that she wanted be a pediatrician when she grew up; consequently, she became a regular ole "box checker" concerned with reaching goals and climbing ladders, hoping to get those same reactions from people on a more consistent basis. She is adamant that her somewhat uptight way of being was not a result of her upbringing, as her parents were very flexible and understanding in their child-rearing tactics, allowing her to do and say things that other (Black) parents subscribing to the rigidness of respectability politics would not fathom or tolerate.

In the first few pages of the memoir, Obama tells readers that her immediate family had never been regular churchgoers, although her aunt and uncle were "prim and serious," as her aunt was an unmovable piano teacher, and her uncle mowed the lawn in suits and wingtips (3). She describes her home as two worlds colliding, her aunt and uncle living in the orderly and mundane space downstairs and her, her mother, father, and brother living in the rowdy and vivacious space upstairs. Reflecting on an event when she talked back to her very serious aunt, Obama notes, "Where another parent might have scolded a kid for being too sassy with an elder," her parents had simply "let it be" (12). As a child, she also drank champagne on New Year's Eve and played sex with her dolls. Her mother talked to her and her brother "like [they] were adults," speaking to them about "drugs and sex and life choices, about race and inequality and politics." She states, "My parents didn't expect us to be saints. My father, I remember, made a point of saying that sex was and should be fun" (25). As a result of their transparency, she was not afraid or ashamed of sexuality. She announced her period "with huge excitement" and proudly "arranged [her] first real kiss" over the phone (48, 50). She also admits that she "fooled around and smoked pot" in her boyfriend's car but took "careful precautions to avoid pregnancy," and when her eighth-grade brother lied about being chaperoned at a girlfriend's house and later confessed, their mother did not get upset or overreact because "it wasn't how she operated" (69, 187, 47). Instead, she insisted that he handle the situation how he thought best. Michelle maintains that every move her mother made "was buttressed by the quiet confidence that she'd raised us to be adults. Our decisions were on us. It was our life, not hers, and always would be" (47). And once Michelle made a few swerves in her career and lifestyle, meaning she threw off the shackles of respectability, it was a life both she and her mother could be proud of.

The swerves in Michelle Obama's life were not brought about on her own accord; they were influenced by people who had made swerving a part of their lifestyles. Swerving, as a byproduct of maverick feminism, involves being in the moment, meeting people where they are, and satisfying self. In addition to her mother, whom she insists "did things her own way," Obama was influenced by many individuals. For instance, she asserts that Barack arrived in her life "a wholly formed person," although she, at that moment, was uncertain and feeling unfilled. He was the "wind that threatened to unsettle everything" (160). Although he was at the top of his law class and had countless job offers, his goals, unlike Michelle's, were not to check off as many boxes as possible and make the most money available. She jokes that during their early courtship, she was not sure if he would ever make any money because he was more concerned about serving other people, and as it is understood, service workers are often not compensated fairly for their deeds. Still, he was self-assured and had his own beliefs, particularly on the institution of marriage.

Where Michelle had come to be a traditionalist in regard to marriage, Barack was anything but and believed that marriage was "an unnecessary and overhyped convention" (114). Since he was not one to be easily suckered by conventions, for several years, they shacked up. When he did propose marriage, it was basically to "shut [her] up." Michelle recalls the proposal: "For a full minute or two, I stared dumbfounded at the ring on my finger. I looked at Barack to confirm that this was all real. He was smiling. He'd completely surprised me. In a way, we'd both won. 'Well,' he said lightly, 'that should shut you up'" (157). They chose a middle ground, or a "modern partnership that suited [them] both." She insists, "He saw marriage as the loving alignment of two people who could lead parallel lives but without forgoing any independent dreams or ambitions." On the other hand, she saw marriage as "a full-on merger, a reconfiguring of two lives into one, with the well-being of a family taking precedence over any one agenda or goal" (140). It appears that what they ultimately contracted is a marriage in which two people navigate life independently but are inseparable in love. As a result, they are happy and fulfilled individuals who can work together as a team to establish and maintain the well-being of the family. This is the way maverick feminism works as well. As I have expressed throughout this text, a maverick feminist is an individual who lives freely, without limitations of conventions, and fulfills self while also uplifting others.

Before and after Barack came into her life and unsettled everything, Michelle was impacted by many women who, likewise, possessed this self-then-society mentality. Santita Jackson, Suzanne Alele, Czerny Braselton, Valerie Jarrett, and Susan Sher were all a part of her becoming. They were nonconventional, multifaceted, and unapologetic women. They were her village, her community, "her safe harbor of female wisdom" (43). And they formed sisterhoods and intergenerational relationships and positively impacted one another's lives.

A couple of the things Michelle admired most about Santita are that "she wore skirts when everyone else wore jeans" and that she was "deep" but could also be "frivolous and goofy." Even more, she appreciated the fact that Santita was "all for strengthening the character of black youth" but also needed to get to the store "before the K-Swiss sneaker sale ended." Finally, she loved that despite the fact that Santita's father was Jesse Jackson, or perhaps precisely because her father was Jesse Jackson, "all she wanted was to be taken on her own terms" (61–65). In essence, Michelle Obama admired the fact that Santita Jackson was a maverick, that she was a part of and devoted to the well-being of the community, but equally devoted to her own self-identity, pleasure, and fulfillment. Michelle herself displayed these same undeniable characteristics to the entire world during her time as First Lady.

In a similar manner, Michelle Obama admired her college roommate, Suzanne, or Screwzy as she affectionately called her, because she had a "lightness of spirit that caused her to stand out among Princeton's studious mass." She was "unafraid to plunge into parties where she didn't know a soul," and did things "for the simple reason that they made her happy." Even as a college-aged girl, Screwzy refused to succumb to her parents' pressure of pursuing a career in medicine simply because doing so "messed with her joy" (75–80). Michelle determines, "She was the Laverne to my Shirley, the Ernie to my Bert. Our shared room resembled an ideological battlefield, with Suzanne presiding over a wrecked landscape of tossed clothing and strewn papers on her side and me perched on my bed, surrounded by fastidious order." Interestingly enough, Michelle seems to be describing her childhood home again, only now she has taken the role of her "prim and serious" aunt. Even the verb choice in this statement is telling. Whereas Suzanne is presiding over, or has control over what appears to be chaos and disorder surrounding her, Michelle is simply perched on her bed, secure but ornamental and not at all in control. She concludes that Suzanne "provoked [her] in a good way, introducing [her] to the idea that not everyone needs to have their file folders labeled and alphabetized, or even have files at all" (80). Suzanne called attention to the mundane and unfulfilling world of respectability politics and reintroduced Michelle to a maverick feminist type of lifestyle, one that may not appear desirable or pristine on the outside but is unrestricting and rewarding on the inside.

Finally, also at Princeton was Czerny, who was, Michelle suggests, "an über-mentor, our ultra-hip and always outspoken defender in chief." She insists that "Czerny saw some sort of potential in me, though I was also clearly short on life experience" (76). Seemingly, Czerny was aware of this lack of experience, and her message to young Michelle was simply "*Get over it and just live a little*" (78). Likewise, although her would-be chief of staff, Susan Sher, is a white woman and could not relate to some of her struggles in the same manner that her mentor, Czerny, could, Michelle notes that her then coworkers, Susan and Valerie, seemed to convey a similar message as Czerny, as they "managed to be both tremendously confident and tremendously human."

As previously noted, while I envision maverick feminism as a praxis specifically for/of Black or African American women, allies of other sexes and races may possess some maverick feminist characteristics, traits that they employ to help mobilize and sustain Black women's maverick feminism. This appears to be the case with Susan; as such, Michelle maintains that, as a *team*, Susan and Valerie "knew their own voices and were unafraid to use them." Likewise, they "could be humorous and humble" and were "unfazed by blowhards" (168). I don't imagine the First Lady can recall or count the egregious number of blowhards that attempted to faze her during her terms in the White House; even if she could, however, she would not care to. Above anything else that she gained from Susan and Valerie, Michelle declares, "They weren't striving for perfect, but managed to somehow always be excellent . . . They'd dropped any masquerade and were just wonderfully, powerfully, and instructively themselves" (168–69). These are the characteristics that we see Michelle display, front and center, at the inauguration of her husband's successor, the characteristics that many blowhards disapproved while Black feminists cheered.

As a result of the impact that each of the above-mentioned ladies—as well as her father and President Obama—had on Michelle's life, she began to shake off her rigidness and live a little, in hopes that her children and future generations of women would do the same. When she learned that she was pregnant with her second child, she suggests that she planned to call her daughter Sasha because "a girl named Sasha would brook no fools" (199). Likewise, upon moving into the White House, she was adamant that her girls did not have to ask permission to go outside to play or to rummage through the pantry for snacks. In other words, they did not need permission to be young and carefree. In fact, one of the things she seems most proud of on Barack's first inauguration day is that during the parade, the girls "were breathless and laughing, having released themselves from all ceremonial dignity. They'd shucked off their hats and messed up each other's hair and were thrashing around, engaged in a sisterly tickle fight. Tired out, finally, they sprawled across the seats and rode the rest of the way with their feet kicked up, blasting Beyoncé on the car stereo as if it were just any old day" (300). Even more intriguing, the former First Lady is irrefutably proud that the "real-life Beyoncé" sang for their first dance at the first inauguration ball (301). She seems proud to assure readers that yes, "they get *it* from their momma," the *it* being unapologetic freeness and an undeniable love for self and culture.

Michelle Obama made it part of her mission as First Lady and beyond to instill and foster this same measure of confidence and individuality in young women of color all over the world. She recollects the leadership and mentoring program she started, facilitating a relationship between girls from greater DC high schools and female White House associates and officials. In summarizing the program, she acknowledges:

> They were smart, curious young women, all of them. No different from me. No different from my daughters. I watched over time as the girls formed friendships, finding a rapport with one another and with the adults around them. I spent hours talking with them in a big circle, munching popcorn and trading our thoughts about college applications, body image, and boys. No topic was off-limits. We ended up laughing a lot. More than anything, I hoped this was what they'd carry forward into the future—the ease, the sense of community, the encouragement to speak and be heard.
>
> My wish for them was the same one I had for Sasha and Malia—that in learning to feel comfortable at the White House, they'd go on to feel comfortable and confident in any room sitting at any table, raising their voices inside any group. (356–57)

This, too, is the goal of maverick feminism: to ascertain that women are self-identified, self-sexualized, and self-actualized. She wanted the young women to be knowledgeable, own their stories, not be rigid, know the importance of community, and not allow their voices to be silenced. These are the same characteristics that were instilled in her by her parents, later smothered by conventions, then revitalized via multiple sisterhoods and intergenerational relationships with women (and a few men) possessing maverick feminist characteristics.

Without a doubt, Michelle Obama's memoir *Becoming* is an exemplar of the positive effects of the intergenerational dynamic, and it supports the notion that Black women often use their lives, their bodies, and their literature as a form of activism. Former assistant director of the White House Initiative on Educational Excellence for African Americans, Lauren Christine Mims, recognizes the importance of

African American women continuing to tell and share their diverse yet universal tales and has used *Becoming* to create a curriculum that will "make space for black girls to thrive in a world that often seems to try and deny their humanity." Furthermore, Mims tells *Black Enterprise* that "there are four things we can all do to support Black girls:

- Create supportive, affirming, and loving environments by listening to their needs and centering their unique experiences of Becoming;
- Advocate for, adopt, and enforce school policies and accountability practices that recognize the brilliance of black girls and ensure they are not being pushed out of school.
- Address the bullying, harassment, and discrimination of black girls and ensure that all students have access to mental healthcare;
- Care for your own mental health and well-being.

This list acknowledges two truths. The first is the grand role adults play in being in community with, advocating for, and being vocal about discrimination against African American girls and women. The second truth is both profoundly simple and simply profound: it is virtually impossible to take care of others without first taking care of self.

Self-care is a privilege that was taken away from Black women during the institution of slavery, as many were pulled from their homes—leaving their own children unprotected—and forced to care for the children of their white owners. However, I argue that our former First Lady's memoir, in conjunction with her recognizable contributions in the lives of young women of color, including her own daughters, is a testament to the necessity of becoming, and of boldly asserting that we now own ourselves and are greatly invested in ours and our children's futures.

CONCLUSION

At the beginning of this chapter, I acknowledged that McMillan's work is perhaps not thought to be on the level as the other texts analyzed in this book. Scholar Gwendolyn Pough (2004) has recognized the success of Terry McMillan's enterprise, noting that she "helped to create a multibillion-dollar market" (70). However, Pough also notes that despite this successful market, little critical attention has been devoted to Black women's text, specifically in the genre of popular fiction. In an attendant fashion, *Getting to Happy* has gained virtually no critical attention from scholars despite the popularity of its prequel and the novel's release more than a decade ago.

Expressing disapproval of McMillan's work immediately after its publication, a reviewer in *Publisher's Weekly* refers to this sequel as a "disappointing and uninspired outing" that the previously adored characters embark on, stating, "The beloved cast isn't given a story worthy of them; instead, this reunion reads like a catalogue of personal catastrophes annotated with very long, rambling discussions, with more emphasis on simple drama than character" (25). Certainly, the novel is not perfect; in fact, portions of the plot are a bit predictable and, indeed, sometimes drawn out, particularly those passages narrated in third person. However, the reviewer seems to be overcome by the mere fact that the characters are overwhelmed with "personal catastrophes," stating, "Within the first few chapters, Gloria and Savannah are struck by disaster, and things go rapidly downhill from there for everyone. Most of the misery has to do with men who lie, steal, cheat, or disappear, or with adult children who face similar problems." This review is akin to those about Walker's *The Color Purple* and Sapphire's *PUSH*, as the reviewer is apparently unenthralled by or uncomfortable with the protagonists' "misery" and resulting development. It fails to acknowledge that this book is not titled *Being Happy*; it is titled *Getting to Happy*, and the process is just as important as the product. Even more, the mere fact that the protagonists deal with the seemingly endless list of catastrophes with their offspring and families is an attempt at ascertaining that the offspring's lives are a little less bleak and drama filled, thereby a bit *more* happy.

In an interview with Gabriel Packard (2012), McMillan insists that an author should "write without looking over [their] shoulder. Write as if no one is going to read it . . . Telling the story," she insists, "hopefully a compelling story, and an emotionally honest story—is more important to me than trying to impress a critic" (24). This, too, is the

CHAPTER THREE

maverick feminist's motto for life. And as illustrated in McMillan's *Getting to Happy* as well as Michelle Obama's *Becoming*, the critic's comfort should never be a primary concern. Whether the critics appreciate the process or not, however, the narratives analyzed in this chapter illustrate that it is virtually impossible to help someone else on their road to becoming if one is not first self-identified, self-sexualized, and/or self-actualized.

CONCLUSION

Progressive art can assist people to learn not only about the
objective forces at work in the society in which they live, but
also about the intensely social character of their interior lives.
Ultimately, it can propel people toward social emancipation.
—ANGELA DAVIS, *WOMEN, CULTURE, AND POLITICS* (1990)

In September 2013, I had the privilege of attending a conference
titled "Unleashing the Black Erotic: Gender and Sexuality (Passion,
Power, and Praxis)," jointly hosted by the College of Charleston's
Avery Research Center for African American History and Culture
and the university's African American Studies Program. At this time,
sexualities studies was still a burgeoning field. Although Patricia Hill
Collins's *Black Sexual Politics: African Americans, Gender, and the New
Racism* (2005) had been published for almost a decade, Stacy Patton's
groundbreaking text, "Who's Afraid of Black Sexuality?" (2012), had
been published only a few months prior to the conference, and scholars all across the globe were engaging the topic, seemingly to answer
Patton's question and say, "Not me; I'm not afraid of Black sexuality."

Among the conference performers and keynote speakers were
E. Patrick Johnson and Joan Morgan. I was elated; I had the opportunity to meet and say a few brief words to my feminist godmother.
While that encounter was a highlight of the conference, I was also
thrilled to hear and see panelists evaluate depictions of Black sexualities (heterosexual and queer) in a range of genres and spaces, including film and television, historically Black colleges, inner cities, the
Caribbean, Hip Hop music and culture, gospel music, poetry, literary
fiction, popular fiction, romance fiction, and strip clubs. By centering

sexuality in a range of Black spaces and places, scholars were engaging in and practicing the tenets of maverick feminism.

One of the most provocative presentations, an essay titled "All I See Is Your Booty Cleavage: Sex and the Contemporary Gospel Song," was presented by Deborah Smith Pollard of the University of Michigan–Dearborn. In the essay, Pollard, a professor of literature and the host and producer of a contemporary gospel music radio program, recognized that some contemporary gospel artists have deliberately incorporated discussions of sex and sexuality into their worship because as they see it, problems of sex and sexuality do not simply go away when one becomes a Christian, rather self-evaluations and critical conversations are imperative to assisting in the holistic improvement of self and Black communities at large. Based on Pollard's analysis, these gospel artists seemed to have recognized that sex and sexuality are inescapable and that attempting to remain virginal, practicing abstinence, or simply avoiding discussions about sex or sexuality is not sufficient action to make the *problem* go away. With this book, I hope that I have conveyed a similar message and added to it that sex and sexuality, inherently, are not a problem at all. Instead, the ways in which African Americans have historically learned about and experienced sex are the problem.

Respectability politics has long since been a matter of accommodating others while neglecting self, and the literary works evaluated in this project unapologetically express the individual and communal detriment that is caused as a result of this neglect. Hurston's Janie, Souljah's Winter, Walker's Celie, Sapphire's Precious, McMillan's Sparrow—none of these girls/women would be considered a *role model*, because they display maverick-like characteristics instead. A maverick is considered an outsider, a person who is unorthodox and unconventional, a nonconformist. A model is an imitation, something/someone that is mass-produced by a system of power. Black feminists such as Anna Julia Cooper, the Combahee River Collective, Audre Lorde, and Angela Davis have, for over a century, urged Black women to "learn not only about the objective forces at work in the society in which they live, but also about the intensely social character of their interior lives." With this book, I have attempted to answer that call and encourage others to do the same.

This interior investigation, like maverick feminism, is selfish and communal simultaneously. As I have argued, it requires one to first become self-identified, self-sexualized, and/or self-actualized before assisting in the liberation and advancement of others. It means jumping off conveyor belts of respectability and no longer encouraging or forcing younger generations to be cleansed and/or (re)manufactured in a similar manner; it means ending the marginalization that takes place within. This theory is a valuable tool both in literature and in life, and as I have demonstrated, many African American women have devoted their literature to this cause in hopes of improving the lives of their communities.

I want to particularly emphasize that this dedication and devotion of one's art toward improving the lives of others moves beyond literary fiction and the academy, as Black women in the popular culture world, too, have consistently participated in the fight. Therefore, I have worked hard to demonstrate the impact that both literature and culture have on the lived experiences of Black women. Each of the chapter titles, as well as some of the section titles, is derived from the song lyrics of Black female Hip Hop artists—Cardi B., Janelle Monáe, and Beyoncé specifically. And each woman has staked her claim in the progression of Black female sexuality and womanhood.

For instance, Janelle Monáe, a queer Black woman, insists that Black womanhood is not monolithic, and in the song "Django Jane" suggests that this desire to see people as a model is a way for oppressors to ban #BlackGirlMagic. She states, "They been trying hard just to make us all vanish / I suggest they put a flag on a whole 'nother planet." Although Monáe has not self-identified as a feminist (because she rejects traditional labels), many of her albums, but specifically *Dirty Computer* (2018), have undeniable feminist characteristics. Freelance writer Derrick Clifton notes that the album *Dirty Computer* "signal[s] a renewed and more emboldened vision of owning and reclaiming power. Monáe's first three albums," he insists, "laid out the code, so that audiences could dream up some tools to reprogram, deprogram and get down. Now, the Electric Lady is leading a clarion call towards a Black, feminist, and queer-inclusive future—one that won't crash or burn." It is important to note that this future in which Monáe envisions and the escape that causes her character Jane to become

Django-esque by the end of the visual album is a result of assistance from a "sister," Mary Apple 53, who has already been presumably cleansed but is reminded by Jane of the joy and passion she experienced before having her individuality erased. A concern of maverick feminism, likewise, is empowering women to work together toward circumventing the crash and burn that results from the simplification and objectification caused by adhering to conventions such as respectability politics.

As I have demonstrated within this book, the "they," described by Monáe, who are insistent on destroying #BlackGirlMagic are no longer limited to white male patriarchy. The Black community, including Black men and other Black feminists, has inflicted damage on itself as well. One only has to say the names of Clarence Thomas and R. Kelly to understand the role that Black men have played in raping, assaulting, and disregarding the lives of Black women. The damage done by other feminists, though, may not be as obvious to some. Here is an example: unlike Janelle Monáe, Beyoncé and Cardi B. have specifically aligned themselves with feminism, but not without discouraging criticism from other feminists. Namely, bell hooks, in a 2016 article, "Moving Beyond Pain," took issue with Beyoncé's *Lemonade* album released earlier that year, insisting that it was a capitalist work not at all dedicated to the empowerment of Black women. hooks suggests that the album promotes violence and pain over self-care and progress.[1] While I agree with hooks that Beyoncé's politics are somewhat problematic, I am willing to bet that, similar to Joan Morgan's argument about popular fiction's dynamic reach, Beyoncé's *Lemonade* and Monáe's *Dirty Computer* reached more young girls and women outside of the academy than Anna Julia Cooper, Audre Lorde, or even Joan Morgan herself ever will. Moreover, contemporary scholars now recognize the violence and pain, as described by hooks, as rage, a natural part of activism and progression.

As I state in my introduction, I wish that I had known when I was growing up, that Hip Hop artists considered themselves feminists. Had the gatekeepers not held such firm notions concerning representation and respectability, I might have joined the mighty chorus long before I was twenty-five. This is why maverick feminism is important. Again, maverick feminism is not a new or revised version of feminism;

instead, maverick feminism is an umbrella term for what many of the most influential Black feminists have been practicing for years. Alice Walker's womanism, Joan Morgan's Hip Hop feminism, and the CFC's crunk feminism are all forms of maverick feminism, as they fulfilled their founders' desires to be feminists but not in the traditional way. These theories fulfilled their desires to satisfy and define self before attempting to theorize to and about others. Specifically, these theories fulfilled their desires to be self-identified, self-sexualized, and self-actualized. These theories also fulfilled their desires to always have access to and be in close proximity with other likeminded Black women. Most importantly, these theories fulfilled *their* desires, not the desires of others.

In case I have not been clear, my aversion to respectability politics is not a promotion of unlawful or immoral practices. And I am in no way encouraging young girls to experience sex at an early age or encouraging them to be promiscuous and proud. Instead, what I am suggesting is that shared knowledge is power. Furthermore, as the text that inspired and spoke life into this entire project, I argue that Hurston's *Their Eyes Were Watching God* disseminates perhaps the most valuable knowledge of all: women do not have to be defined by or succumb to old customs when their dreams are on further horizons. This bit of knowledge did not bode well with Hurston's contemporaries because they did not see space for both a Black renaissance and a Black woman's renaissance; however, it resonates with contemporary women. If engaged in a critical and personal manner, this practice (and Hurston's text) can be especially relatable to younger generations, particularly Gen Z-ers who pride themselves on the ideas of independence, self-definition, and self-sexualization, qualities depicted by Hurston's protagonist, Janie, and, arguably, by Hurston herself. Many suggest that Hurston was ahead of her time; the more suitable estimation, however, is that she was a maverick while others wanted her to be a model.

I have insisted throughout this work that respectability politics is a debilitating and fruitless endeavor, as it further marginalizes the often already discriminated against and reduces the likelihood of everyday Black people having both promising and fulfilling lives. I hope to see more scholarship from Black feminists and literary and

cultural studies scholars who acknowledge that while the initial violence inflicted on the Black (female) body was no fault of our own,
future violence inflicted on the Black (female) body, likewise, ought
not come at the hands and ideologies (or lack thereof) of other African Americans.

Trimiko Melancon in *Unbought and Unbossed: Transgressive Black
Women, Sexuality, and Representation* (2014) and Traci D. O'Neal in
*The Exceptional Negro: Racism, White Privilege and the Lie of Respect-
ability Politics* (2018) have already begun engaging contemporary
effects of respectability politics, particularly on Black women. And
University of Alabama professor Cassander Smith argues in her book
Race and Respectability in an Early Black Atlantic that respectability
politics was used to no avail by Black Africans as early as the eigh-
teenth century and, hence, is "a fool's errand." Works such as Glory
Edim's *Well-Read Black Girl* (2018), adrienne maree brown's *Pleasure Activism* (2019), and Mikki Kendall's *Hood Feminism* (2020)
are also vital to this conversation and movement, as they move the
Black woman, along with her body, stories, deeds, and pleasures, from
margins to center and reiterate the importance of both individuality
and solidarity. I imagine that the more we encounter these radical
truths, the less we will endorse prescribed notions, and, therefore, the
less we will promote the self-effacing and self-deprecating practices
taught to the Black race by men who attempted, achieved, and continuously aspire to our enslavement. Likewise, as previously stated,
the more we teach Black girls and women (and women of all races)
to be unapologetically aware and possessive of their own bodies, the
less power other people, particularly violent men and proponents of
respectability politics, will have over them.

I began writing this book pondering how I could add to the fields
of literature and gender and sexualities studies while simultaneously
extending the discussions and strides made by the Black Lives Matter
movement, and I came to the conclusion that activism has never been
limited to picket signs, protests, marches, riots, or traditional political
work. Enslavers have always feared the written word. The written word
has the power to cultivate and free an entire nation of people. The
narratives of freed and escaped slaves propelled the abolitionist movement. The impeccable journalistic skills of Ida B. Wells catapulted the

antilynching movement. The sophisticated pedagogy of Anna Julia Cooper spurred the suffrage movement. And the boisterous speeches of Fannie Lou Hamer anchored the civil rights movement. All the while, from behind the scenes, Black women have offered their narratives, both fiction and nonfiction, in contribution to the fight. This book is praise for and testament to their impact.

So, no, I do not agree with Kenneth Warren's claim that African American literature no longer exists simply because the impetus for African American literature's rise as a national literature—Jim Crow and legalized discrimination and segregation—is no more. Jane Crow and unlawful separation, sexualization, and discrimination have not waned. And neither have the voices of Black women. They simply have taken on multiple new forms. After all, the Black Lives Matter and #MeToo movements gained momentum on social media. Roxanne Fequiere notes that Tomi Adeyemi, Akwaeke Emezi, Elizabeth Acevedo, Angie Thomas, and Nic Stone are "voices of change" who are "rewriting the rules of young adult fiction." Angie Thomas adds veracity to this claim when she tells *People*, in an exclusive interview about her book *Concrete Rose*, released in January 2021, that she absolutely expects her new book to be banned because no one wants to talk about teenage sex and teenage pregnancy. Though she insists, "Your discomfort is not my problem. My concern is for those young people who need this book." I argue that it is not just the young people who need these types of books, however. Equally so, it is not just the young people who need maverick feminism, sisterhoods, and intergenerational relationships.

We can all benefit from the sharing of narratives that are both unapologetically Black and unapologetically self-sexualized. It is my greatest hope that this book will provoke the writings, thoughts, and conversations of others, both in and outside of the academy, so that we can nurture a race of people who truly understand what Audre Lorde meant when she said that "it is axiomatic that if we do not define ourselves for ourselves, we will be defined by others—for their use and to our detriment" (45). What we lose when we do not define ourselves, in addition to freedom, is pleasure. Sami Schalk insists, "Sometimes in the academy, there is a suggestion that pleasure and intellectual work cannot combine, that our work is only recognizable if it is hard, if it exhausts us. Sometimes in feminism and social justice movements, there is the suggestion that increased political awareness reduces one's ability to take pleasure in cultural awareness" (143). In this project, I have tried to merge the two worlds, the political and the pleasurable. And I confess that while the task of writing and publishing this book did become exhausting at times, I always found pleasure in my Black womanhood, whether intellectually, socially, or sensually.

Before I end this book, I have to admit that I did not grow up reading the works of Zora Neale Hurston, Toni Morrison, Alice Walker, or any of the authors analyzed in this study. I can't even say that I read the likes of *The Baby-Sitters Club* or any other adolescent fiction of the time. And I encountered very few representations of Black womanhood on television, outside of those depicted on BET (Black Entertainment Television). Until my adult conversion to Black feminism, my female-dominated family was a main source for sisterhood and community, and rightfully so. However, Black girls today have so many options, and I hope that we continue to give them even more. The year 2019 was an unprecedented one for Black women: Miss America, Miss Teen USA, Miss USA, and Miss Universe were all Black women. Likewise, the first female vice president of the United States is a Black woman. I took and still take great pleasure in these truths and deem them a victory for all Black women. But I also realize that there is still more work to do. Ultimately, Black women, and by and large, the Black community, will only be both free and fulfilled when we relinquish the strongholds of respectability politics and no longer subscribe to the caricatures placed before the Black race by sixteenth- and seventeenth-century European explorers and colonialists who undoubtedly saw the gold mines living within our bodies and desperately hoped that we never would. It's time to take back and reclaim our everything!

ACKNOWLEDGMENTS

This book has been a work in progress for many years. I have changed and grown so much since its conception. Black feminisms and gender and sexualities studies have changed and grown so much since its conception. Unfortunately, the world—and its treatment of Black girls and women—has not changed much at all. This is the problem I wanted to highlight in my book.

First, thank you to all of my mentors and colleagues who played a part, large or small, in helping me see this project through to the end. Special shoutout to Dr. Cassie Smith for providing me with sample drafts and for reading my drafts. Thank you for your never-ending support and mentorship, for offering encouraging words as well as criticism, for giving it to me straight, and for cheering me on every step of the way. Thanks especially to my department chairs at Gardner-Webb University for working with my crazy scheduling requests so that I could have time to read, write, and revise. Thanks also to Drs. June Hobbs and Shea Stuart for reading early drafts and offering the best feedback and support. To Dr. Janet Land, thanks for continuing to host Writing Across the Curriculum (WAC) and for always having a place for me at the Wild Acres retreat. That unadulterated writing time each year was more valuable than you know. Again, thank you all. I am honored to work with and learn from each of you.

To my best girlfriends, Drs. Kedra James and Delia Steverson and soon to be Dr. Brittney Bates, thank you for being you, for embodying the true meaning of sisterhood. I know that I am the nonchalant one of the group, but your eagerness and excitement for my accomplishments never go unnoticed or unappreciated. I am grateful for each of you being bold and unapologetic in your own way. Special thank you to Kedra for being an awesome roommate and writing buddy, for reading drafts and offering feedback, and for having my back since undergrad. I truly do love y'all.

To my family, I am so glad God chose you for me. You embody dignity; you embody grit. You embody politeness; you embody sass. You embody love; you embody strength. I am proud to be a part of you. Thank you for supporting me. Special shout-out to my aunts, the "famous" Givens Girls. You continue to be a link in the chain of my own maverick feminism.

To my parents and siblings, thank you for making me believe that a girl from the Mississippi Delta could do and be anything she wanted to be. To my dad, who always wanted the best for me and has been my protector from day one, thank you for loving me, even when I rebelled against every rule you ever set. To my mom, I could never thank you for all the things you have done for and taught me; my earliest memory of you is you taking back what rightfully belonged to you, and I will always be most proud of that. You have always been my pillar, my friend, my cheerleader, and it makes me proud just to know that you are proud. I am who I am because you are who you are. Family, I love you all.

Thank you to my husband, Jason, for supporting me in many ways throughout this process, especially during the final stretch. I never realized how difficult it would be to try to write a book and be a full-time professor, wife, and mother and still make time for me and all the other things I did before I became a professor, wife, and mother. But you lightened the load where you could and made me smile every day. Thank you. I love you.

Lastly, to my sweet Jayden, my next generation: Thank you for teaching me the true meaning of unconditional love and happiness. I wish that I could hold you in my arms forever, but since you have nearly outgrown me, and holding you is, now, virtually impossible, I promise to do my best to make sure that you know what to take from this world and what to give it. I love you and will always be your biggest cheerleader and advocate.

NOTES

INTRODUCTION: RECLAIMING MY EVERYTHING: BLACK FEMINISMS, POPULAR CULTURE, AND PLEASURE

1. This quote is, of course, a play on words as Audre Lorde, like the Lord (God), is considered by many as a savior. Also, this quote is in reference to a similar refrain used by the Summer of Our Lorde Study Group in 2008.

2. *Boughetto* is a combination of the terms *bougie* and *ghetto*, suggesting that a person has middle- or high-class values with a hood background or upbringing.

3. The account of Vespucci's voyage, reportedly taken place between 1499 and 1500, is documented in Sebastian Münster's *A Treatyse of the New India* and was translated to English by Richard Eden in 1553. Gainsh's account is documented in Richard Eden and Richard Willes's 1577 publication *The History of Travayle in the West and East Indies*.

4. I say *seemed* here because without even knowing the circumstances of her situation, the assumption that many would make about Colvin's resultant pregnancy is that she was yet another licentious Black youth who could not control her sexual desires. And while it was thought that the NAACP was attempting to shield her from public humiliation, shielding and forgetting are not equivalent. Colvin's eventual move to New York after the birth of her child is but one indication that she could have benefitted greatly from maverick feminist support.

5. Cooper defines *embodied discourse* as a "form of Black female textual activism wherein race women assertively demand the inclusion of their bodies and, in particular, working-class bodies and Black female bodies by placing them in the texts they write and speak" (3).

6. For further analysis and discussion, see Grimké's "To My Father upon His Fifty-Fifth Birthday" and other poems, along with Carolivia Herron's "The Introduction to *The Selected Works of Angelina Weld Grimké*" (1991).

7. Several days after advocating for the rights and fair treatment of AIDS victims and admitting in an interview that she had been HIV positive for two years, on July 6, 1992, Johnson's body was found floating in the Hudson River, and the

death was ruled a suicide. However, acts of foul play have been suggested, and the case remains open.

8. In 2016, the United States Department of Health and Human Services Office of Minority Health shared the following statistics: "1.) Adult Black/African Americans are 20 percent more likely to report serious psychological distress than adult whites, 2.) Adult Black/African Americans living below poverty are three times more likely to report serious psychological distress than those living above poverty, and 3.) Adult Black/African Americans are more likely to have feelings of sadness, hopelessness, and worthlessness than are adult whites." The Office of Minority Health acknowledges that these psychological disparities are due to continued racism as well as mistreatment by and mistrust of authority figures, leaving African Americans seeking other coping mechanisms. The politics of respectability has long since been one of those coping mechanisms, but as African Americans are averse to traditional coping mechanisms such as seeking psychological counseling (also due to mistrust and other stigmas around weakness), respectability as a coping mechanism does little to alleviate problems and instead adds to them. Furthermore, the Anxiety and Depression Association of America insists that "for Black women, anxiety is more chronic and the symptoms more intense than their White counterparts [as a result of] how Black women are viewed in this country . . . Research and history tell us that three basic images exist—the Strong Black Woman, the Angry Black Woman, and the Jezebel/Video Vixen. These images affect how other people see Black women and how they see themselves. They also play a role in the development and maintenance of anxiety." This article was published April 23, 2018.

CHAPTER ONE:
DIRTY COMPUTER: GIRLHOOD AND SEXUAL DESIRES

1. See brown, *Pleasure Activism*.

2. These types of realities are the reasons why intergenerational dynamics are valuable, both in life and in literature. Although motherhood, for women, is often thought of as a consequence of expressed sexuality, readers do not get the impression that Janie is susceptible to pregnancy. Over six decades later, however, this possibility is made very clear to Sister Souljah's Winter, as she is prescribed birth control pills at an early age and yet finds herself impregnated. Referring to contemporary generations and including herself in the group, Joan Morgan insists, "We walk through the world with a sense of entitlement that women of our mothers' generation could not begin to fathom. Most of us can't imagine our lives without access to birth control, legalized abortions, the right to vote, or

many of the same educational and job opportunities available to men" (59). Janie's beauty and sexuality are what grant her the attention and support of wealthy men who make it possible to survive without equal education or occupation, but beauty and sexuality do not suppress pregnancy. In fact, beauty and sexuality were contributing factors to Winter's pregnancy. Yes, she "handles" the pregnancy by using her generational entitlement to abortion, but Janie is more privileged than Winter in this case because she is allowed to express her sexuality without fear of an unwanted pregnancy. How might Pheoby have felt about Janie had Janie divulged that she did have a daughter left alone somewhere on the muck? How might supportive readers' opinions of her change? Is Winter less respectable for using her privilege? While it is arguable that Janie was not privileged at all and was in fact sterile instead, all in all, these examples are meant to suggest that topics of pregnancy, abortion, or contraception are unlikely when discussing *Their Eyes* in isolation, but pairing the text with a more contemporary work adds depth to its analytical possibilities.

On a similar note, despite the fact that Janie's character existed in the early 1900s, she is noted for having "left" more than one husband and for having a hefty sexual appetite, attributes that have made her and her author a main staple in (African) American (women's) literature today. However, not once is a contraceptive mentioned amid Janie's freely expressed and experienced sexual encounters. This gives readers the impression that women, or people in general, during this period of time were immune to sexually transmitted diseases. But while physicians have been privy to knowledge of AIDS only since the late 1970s to early '80s, the Tuskegee syphilis experiment is evidence that sexually transmitted diseases such as syphilis and gonorrhea were indeed prevalent during Hurston's, and therefore Janie's, time. When one uses the intergenerational dynamic, a lineal discussion can be made between *Their Eyes Were Watching God* and *The Coldest Winter Ever* to determine why an issue as serious as disease was frivolous or irrelevant at one point in history but was and is a major campaign in the twentieth and twenty-first centuries. In fact, Souljah appears as a character in *The Coldest Winter Ever* that speaks at a women's prison facility to a wing of women who are all HIV-positive, stating that women often become so consumed with men, love, and sex that "we [often] forget to strengthen our minds so that we can learn how to think, how to build. How to survive. We forget how to live our lives to protect our spirit, to be clean and decent. We forget that everything we do matters so much" (272–73). In other words, we forget to be self-identified, self-actualized, and self-sexualized.

3. An argument could be made that Janie's blooming season had passed. However, as she is only in her late forties when she returns to Eatonville, she is still a ripe age to express her sexuality. Moreover, this would equate to an ageist and one-sided argument.

4. In their mission statement, published in 2010, the Crunk Feminist Collective insists that "the term 'crunk' was initially coined from a contraction of 'crazy' or 'chronic' (weed) and 'drunk' and was used to describe a state of uberintoxication, where a person is 'crazy drunk,' out of their right mind, and under the influence. But where merely getting crunk signaled that you were out of your mind, a crunk feminist mode of resistance will help you *get your mind right.*" See their blog-turned-book titled *The Crunk Feminist Collection* (2017).

CHAPTER TWO: BE CAREFUL WITH ME:
EDUCATION, SEXUAL VIOLENCE, AND PLEASURE

1. See Aliyyah Abdur-Rahman's *Against the Closet: Black Political Longing and the Erotics of Race* (2012) and Candice Jenkins's "Queering Black Patriarchy: The Salvific Wish and Masculine Possibility in Alice Walker's *The Color Purple*" (2002).
2. While some critics may view the choir director and lead singer in the film as Shug's potential mother and daughter respectively, these suppositions are not made as explicit as the fact that the reverend is indeed the father whom Shug *must* please.
3. In *The Kid* (2011), the sequel to *PUSH*, Rita also has brief custody of Abdul after Precious dies, although there is suspicion that she altered the name on his records so that she could continue receiving assistance for him while he is in foster care. Despite this implied deceitfulness, their relationship was seen by others as significant enough for Rita to look after Precious's child.
4. In relation to food customs, it is interesting to note that Precious's meal is considered a southern tradition. In the novel, we learn that her mother and grandmother are originally from Greenwood, Mississippi, and, like many Black southerners, migrated to the North in hopes of better opportunities.
5. Harpo and Sofia, secondary characters in *The Color Purple*, are also an example of how food is thought to influence one's sexuality. Harpo eats excessively, hoping to gain weight and be manly enough to control and ultimately beat his wife, Sofia. He fails, however, and Sofia is continuously the dominant one; "She not quite as tall as Harpo but much bigger, and strong and ruddy looking, like her mama brought her up on pork," ham perhaps (31).

CHAPTER THREE:
GET IN FORMATION: SISTERHOOD AND THE
INTERGENERATIONAL DYNAMIC

1. Oprah Winfrey is an African American most noted for her inspirational and influential talk show, *The Oprah Winfrey Show*. Annie Oakley, born in Ohio

in 1860, was an American sharpshooter, of English descent, until her health declined in 1925 and her eventual death in 1926. Oprah promoted education and personal well-being; Annie starred in violent Western shows and was implicated in a cocaine scandal. Sparrow is a combination of the two: intuitive, caring, and influential, yet brave and nonconformist.

2. Sparrow gives Robin a similar explanation, stating, "I'm not running from anything. I haven't had anything tragic happen to me yet, so I'm cool with my own head" (22). When she makes this statement, Sparrow does not yet recognize not having a father as being potentially "tragic," but it is clear that both she and Taylor lack the ideal family upbringing. Because Sparrow has always had her mother, her sentiments of living with a single parent may be different from a young girl who does not have this motherly figure. Either way, the two girls decide against allowing ensuing restrictions and oppressors to dictate their lives.

3. Rona Barrett is a Caucasian American born in New York in 1936. She is most noted for her gossip column that was popularized during the 1960s; she currently runs a nonprofit organization dedicated to providing affordable living and services to senior citizens.

4. The order of character analysis is designed according to the significance of mother-daughter relationship: Robin and Sparrow are actual mother and daughter, Taylor is Bernadine's stepdaughter, Gloria skips a generation and makes a special connection with her grandchildren, and Savannah does not have offspring, so she, in turn, has to forge and strengthen a relationship with her equal and the generation before her.

CONCLUSION

1. It was during the close of the year 2013 when feminists began paying especially close attention to Beyoncé, as she self-identified as feminist in her self-titled album and in the song "Flawless," used a voiceover of Nigerian novelist and feminist Chimamanda Ngozi Adichie, spelling out society's gender issues and her own personal definition of a feminist.

WORKS CITED

ABS-CBN Entertainment. "The Winning Answer of Miss Universe 2019 Zozibini Tunzi | Miss Universe 2019." *YouTube*, December 8, 2019, 0:30–0:57. www .youtube.com/watch?v=goUiXVbpvgg.

Adamson, Joni. "Spiky Green Life: Environmental, Food, and Sexual Justice Themes in *PUSH*." *Sapphire's Literary Breakthrough: Erotic Literacies, Feminist Pedagogies, Environmental Justice Perspectives*, edited by Elizabeth McNeil et al., Palgrave MacMillan, 2012, pp. 69–88.

Bambara, Toni Cade. "On the Issue of Roles." 1970. *The Black Woman: An Anthology*, edited by Toni Cade Bambara, Washington Square Press, 2005, pp. 123–36.

Baraka, Amiri. "Expressive Language." 1963. *Home: Social Essays*. Akashic Books, 2009, pp. 190–95.

Bloom, Harold, et al. *Modern Critical Views: Alice Walker*. Chelsea House Publishers, 1989.

Bobo, Jacqueline. "Black Women's Responses to *The Color Purple*." *Jump Cut*, no. 33, 1988, pp. 43–51, www.ejumpcut.org/archive/onlinessays/JC33folder /ClPurpleBobo.html.

brown, adrienne maree. *Pleasure Activism: The Politics of Feeling Good*. AK Press, 2019.

Burrell, Christopher, and James Wermers. "Why Does *Precious* Have to Lighten Up to Shuffle? Teaching with Lee Daniel's 'Adaptation.'" *Sapphire's Literary Breakthrough: Erotic Literacies, Feminist Pedagogies, Environmental Justice Perspectives*, edited by Elizabeth McNeil et al., Palgrave MacMillan, 2012, pp. 211–25.

Carby, Hazel V. "It Jus Be's Dat Way Sometime: The Sexual Politics of Women's Blues." 1986. *The Jazz Cadence of American Culture*, edited by Robert G. O'Meally, Columbia University Press, 1998, pp. 469–82.

Carby, Hazel V. *Reconstructing Womanhood: The Emergence of the Afro-American Woman Novelist*. Oxford University Press, 1987.

Cavanaugh, Laurie A. Review of *Getting to Happy*, by Terry McMillan. *Library Journal*, July 2010, p. 76.

Chiles, Nick. "Their Eyes Were Reading Smut." *New York Times*, January 4, 2006, www.nytimes.com/2006/01/04/opinion/their-eyes-were-reading -smut.html.

Christian, Barbara. *Black Women Novelists: The Development of Tradition.* Greenwood Press, 1980.

Christian, Barbara. "The Highs and Lows of Black Feminist Criticism." *Reading Black, Reading Feminist: A Critical Anthology,* edited by Henry Louis Gates Jr., Meridian Books, 1990, pp. 44–51.

Clarke, Deborah. "The Porch Couldn't Talk for Looking: Voice and Vision in *Their Eyes Were Watching God.*" *African American Review,* vol. 35, no. 4, 2001, pp. 599–613.

Clifton, Derrick. "Janelle Monáe's 'Dirty Computer' Delivers a Black, Feminist, and Queer Vision of Freedom." *Them,* April 14, 2018, www.them.us/story /janelle-monaes-dirty-computer-delivers-a-black-feminist-and-queer -vision-of-freedom.

Coates, Ta-Nehisi. *Between the World and Me.* Spiegel and Grau, 2015.

Collins, Patricia Hill. *Black Feminist Thought: Knowledge, Consciousness, and the Politics of Empowerment.* Routledge, 1990.

Collins, Patricia Hill. *Black Sexual Politics: African Americans, Gender, and the New Racism.* Routledge, 2005.

Collins, Patricia Hill. *Fighting Words: Black Women and the Search for Justice.* University of Minnesota Press, 1998.

Coly, Ayo A. "A Pedagogy of the Black Female Body: Viewing Angèle Essamaba's Black Female Nudes." *Third Text,* vol. 24, no. 6, 2010, pp. 653–64.

Cooper, Brittney. *Beyond Respectability: The Intellectual Thought of Race Women.* University of Illinois Press, 2017.

Cooper, Brittney. "Disrespectability Politics: On Jay-Z's Bitch, Beyoncé's 'Fly' Ass, and Black Girl Blue." *Crunk Feminist Collective,* January 19, 2012, www.crunk feministcollective.com/2012/01/19/disrespectability-politics-on-jay-zs-bitch -beyonces-fly-ass-and-black-girl-blue/.

Cooper, Brittney. *Eloquent Rage: A Black Feminist Discovers Her Superpower.* St. Martin's Press, 2018.

Crunk Feminist Collective. "Hip Hop Generation Feminism: A Manifesto." March 1, 2010, www.crunkfeministcollective.com/2010/03/01/hip-hop -generation-feminism-a-manifesto/.

Crunk Feminist Collective. "Mission Statement." 2010, www.crunkfeministcollec tive.com/about/.

Dickerson, Bette, and Nicole Rosseau. "Ageism through Omission: The Obsolescence of Black Women's Sexuality." *Journal of African American Studies,* vol. 13, no. 3, 2009, pp. 307–24.

Donaldson, Elizabeth. "Handing Back Shame: Incest and Sexual Confession in
  Sapphire's *PUSH*." *Transgression and Taboo: Critical Essays*, edited by Vartin P.
  Messier and Nandita Batra, College English Association, 2005, pp. 51–60.

duCille, Anne. *The Coupling Convention: Sex, Text, and Tradition in Black
  Women's Fiction*. Oxford University Press, 1993.

Dyson, Michael Eric. Cover endorsement. *Eloquent Rage: A Black Feminist
  Discovers Her Superpower*, by Brittney Cooper, St. Martin's Press, 2018.

Edim, Glory. *Well-Read Black Girl: Finding Our Stories, Discovering Ourselves*.
  Ballantine Books, 2018.

Fequiere, Roxanne. "Voices of Change." *Elle*, February 3, 2020, www.elle.com
  /culture/books/a30612269/young-adult-fiction-authors-interview/.

Ferguson, Otis. "You Can't Hear Their Voices." *New Republic*, October 13, 1937.
  Zora Neale Hurston: Critical Perspectives Past and Present. Edited by Henry
  Louis Gates Jr. and K. A. Appiah, Amistad Press, 1993.

Fulton, DoVeanna S. "Looking for 'the Alternative[s]': Locating Sapphire's
  PUSH in African American Literary Tradition through Literacy and Orality."
  *Sapphire's Literary Breakthrough: Erotic Literacies, Feminist Pedagogies,
  Environmental Justice Perspectives*, edited by Elizabeth McNeil et al., Palgrave
  MacMillan, 2012, pp. 161–70.

Fultz, Lucille P. *Toni Morrison: Playing with Difference*. University of Illinois Press,
  2003.

Gates, Henry Louis, Jr. "Why Richard Wright Hated Zora Neale Hurston." *The
  Root*, March 18, 2013, www.theroot.com/why-richard-wright-hated-zora
  -neale-hurston-1790895606.

Gay, Roxane. *Hunger: A Memoir of (My) Body*. HarperCollins, 2017.

Ginsberg, Gab. "Janelle Monáe on Owning Her Queer Identity with 'Dirty Computer':
  'It's Important to Speak from That Perspective.'" *Billboard*, August 29, 2018,
  www.billboard.com/articles/columns/pop/8472705/janelle-monae-interview
  -dirty-computer-tour.

Griffin, Farah Jasmine. "That Our Mothers May Soar and the Daughters May
  Know Their Names: A Retrospective of Black Feminist Literary Criticism."
  2007. *Still Brave: The Evolution of Black Women Studies*, edited by Stanlie M.
  James et al., Feminist Press, 2009, pp. 336–60.

Hammonds, Evelynn. "Black (W)holes and the Geometry of Black Female
  Sexuality." *differences: A Journal of Feminist Cultural Studies*, vol. 6, no. 2–3,
  1994, pp. 126–45.

Harris, Fredrick C. *The Price of the Ticket: Barack Obama and the Rise and Decline
  of Black Politics*. Oxford University Press, 2012.

Harris, Trudier. "On *The Color Purple*, Stereotypes, and Silence." *Black American
  Literature Forum*, vol. 18, no. 4, 1984, pp. 155–61.

Herron, Carolivia, ed. *Selected Works of Angelina Weld Grimké*. Oxford University Press, 1991.

Hibben, Sheila. "Vibrant Book Full of Nature and Salt." *New York Herald Tribune Weekly Book Review*, September 26, 1937. *Zora Neale Hurston: Critical Perspectives Past and Present*. Edited by Henry Louis Gates Jr. and K. A. Appiah, Amistad Press, 1993.

Higginbotham, Evelyn Brooks. *Righteous Discontent: The Women's Movement in the Black Baptist Church, 1880–1920*. Harvard University Press, 1993.

Hine, Darlene Clark. "Rape and the Inner Lives of Black Women in the Middle West." *Signs*, vol. 14, no. 4, 1989, pp. 912–20.

Hite, Molly. "Romance, Marginality, and Matrilineage: *The Color Purple* and *Their Eyes Were Watching God*." *Reading Black, Reading Feminist: A Critical Anthology*, edited by Henry Louis Gates Jr., Meridan Books, 1990, pp. 431–53.

hooks, bell. "Moving Beyond Pain." bell hooks Institute. May 9, 2016, www.bell hooksinstitute.com/blog/2016/5/9/moving-beyond-pain.

hooks, bell. "Writing the Subject: Reading *The Color Purple*." *Reading Black, Reading Feminist: A Critical Anthology*, edited by Henry Louis Gates Jr., Meridan Books, 1990, pp. 454–70.

Hoose, Phillip. *Claudette Colvin: Twice Towards Justice*. Square Fish, 2019.

Hughes, Langston. "The Negro Artist and the Racial Mountain." 1926. *African American Literary Theory: A Reader*, edited by Winston Napier, New York University Press, 2000, pp. 27–30.

Hull, Gloria. T. *Color, Sex, and Poetry: Three Women Writers of the Harlem Renaissance*. Indiana University Press, 1987.

Hunter, Tera. *To 'Joy My Freedom: Southern Black Women's Lives and Labor after the Civil War*. Harvard University Press, 1997.

Hurston, Zora Neale. "Art and Such." 1938. *Reading Black, Reading Feminist: A Critical Anthology*, edited by Henry Louis Gates Jr., Meridian Books, 1990, pp. 21–26.

Hurston, Zora Neale. *Their Eyes Were Watching God*. 1937. HarperCollins, 2010.

Jenkins, Candice M. *Black Bourgeois: Class and Sex in the Flesh*. University of Minnesota Press, 2019.

Jenkins, Candice M. *Private Lives, Proper Relations: Regulating Black Intimacy*. University of Minnesota Press, 2007.

Jenkins, Candice M. "Queering Black Patriarchy: The Salvific Wish and Masculine Possibility in Alice Walker's *The Color Purple*." *MFS Modern Fiction Studies*, vol. 48 no. 4, 2002, pp. 969–1000. *Project MUSE*, doi:10.1353/mfs.2002.0075.

Jones, Gayl. *Corregidora*. 1975. Beacon Press, 1986.

Jones, LaMont, Jr. "Endless Exodus: Faculty of Color Leave the Academy in Search of Fulfillment." *Diverse Issues in Higher Education*, vol. 36, no. 11, 2019, www

.questia.com/magazine/1G1-594925279/endless-exodus-faculty-of-color-leave
-the-academy.

Jones, Tayari. "Literature at the Crossroads." *eJournal USA*, vol. 14, no. 2, February
2009, pp. 7–9.

Kaplan, Carla. "The Erotics of Talk: That Oldest Human Longing in *Their Eyes
Were Watching God*." *American Literature*, vol. 67, no. 1, March 1995, pp. 115–42.

Kaplan, Carla, ed. *Zora Neale Hurston: A Life in Letters*. Doubleday, 2002.

Kendall, Mikki. *Hood Feminism: Notes from the Women that a Movement Forgot*.
Viking, 2020.

Kincaid, Jamaica. "Jamaica Kincaid on Writing, Her Life, and *The New Yorker*."
Chicago Humanities Festival, 2014, www.chicagohumanities.org/media
/jamaica-kincaid-writing-her-life-and-new-yorker/.

Lee, Chana Kai. *For Freedom's Sake: The Life of Fannie Lou Hamer*. University of
Illinois Press, 1999.

Lee, Shayne. *Erotic Revolutionaries: Black Women, Sexuality, and Popular Culture*.
Hamilton Books, 2010.

Lester, Neal A. "Rock the Motherfucking House: Guiding a Study of Sapphire's
PUSH." *Sapphire's Literary Breakthrough: Erotic Literacies, Feminist Pedagogies,
Environmental Justice Perspectives*, edited by Elizabeth McNeil et al., Palgrave
MacMillan, 2012, pp. 183–210.

Ligon, Richard. *A True and Exact History of the Island of Barbados*. 1657. Hackett
Publishing, 2011.

Locke, Alain. Review of *Their Eyes Were Watching God*, by Zora Neale Hurston.
Opportunity, June 1, 1938. *Zora Neale Hurston: Critical Perspectives Past and
Present*. Edited by Henry Louis Gates Jr. and K. A. Appiah, Amistad Press,
1993.

Lorde, Audre. "Scratching the Surface: Some Notes on Barriers to Women and
Loving." 1978. *Sister Outsider: Essays and Speeches*. Crossing Press, 1984,
pp. 45–52.

Marshall, Elizabeth, et. al. "Ghetto Fabulous: Reading Black Adolescent Femininity
in Contemporary Urban Street Fiction." *Journal of Adolescent and Adult
Literacy*, vol. 53, no. 1, 2009, pp. 28–36.

Masters, William H., et al. *Human Sexuality*, 5th ed., Addison-Wesley Longman,
1995.

McElya, Micki. *Clinging to Mammy: The Faithful Slave in Twentieth-Century
America*. Harvard University Press, 2007.

McKay, Nellie. "Crayon Enlargements of Life: Zora Neale Hurston's *Their Eyes
Were Watching God* as Autobiography." *New Essays on Their Eyes Were
Watching God*, edited by Michael Awkward, Cambridge University Press,
1990, pp. 51–70.

McMillan, Terry. *Getting to Happy*. Viking, 2011.

Michlin, Monica. "Narrative as Empowerment: *Push* and the *Signifying* on Prior African-American Novels on Incest." *Études Anglaises*, vol. 59, no. 2, 2006, pp. 170–85.

Mills, Kay, and Marian Wright Edelman. *This Little Light of Mine: The Life of Fannie Lou Hamer*. University of Kentucky Press, 2007.

Monáe, Janelle. *Dirty Computer*. Bad Boy Records, 2018.

Morgan, Jennifer L. "Some Could Suckle over Their Shoulder: Male Travelers, Female Bodies, and the Gendering of Racial Ideology, 1500–1770." *William and Mary Quarterly*, Third Series, vol. 54, no. 1, 1997, pp. 167–92.

Morgan, Joan. *When Chickenheads Come Home to Roost: A Hip-Hop Feminist Breaks It Down*. Touchstone, 2000.

Morgan, Joan. "Why We Get Off: Moving Towards a Black Feminist Politics of Pleasure." *Black Scholar*, vol. 45, no. 4, 2015, pp. 36–46.

Morrison, Toni. *Playing with Darkness: Whiteness and the Literary Imagination*. Vintage Books, 1993.

Morrison, Toni. *Sula*. Alfred A. Knopf, 1973.

Nadeem, Tania. "Review of *The Coldest Winter Ever*." *Journal of the American Academy of Child and Adolescent Psychiatry*, vol. 49, no. 1, 2010, pp. 85–86.

Naylor, Gloria. "Love and Sex in the Afro-American Novel." *Yale Review*, vol. 78, no. 1, 1989, pp. 19–31.

Obama, Michelle. *Becoming*. Crown, 2018.

Packard, Gabriel. "Writing Like No One Is Looking [Interview]." *Writer*, vol. 125, no. 2, 2012, p. 24.

Palmieri, Carl "Tuchy." *Oprah, In Her Words: Our American Princess*. BookSurge, 2008.

Patton, Stacey. "Who's Afraid of Black Sexualities?" *Chronicle of Higher Education: The Chronicle Review*, December 3, 2012, https://www.chronicle.com/article/whos-afraid-of-black-sexuality/.

Pough, Gwendolyn D. *Check It While I Wreck It: Black Womanhood, Hip Hop Culture, and the Public Sphere*. Northeastern University Press, 2004.

Quashie, Kevin. *Black Women, Identity, and Cultural Theory*. Rutgers University Press, 2004.

Randle, Kemeshia. "Gang Wars: The Academy vs. the Street." *Street Lit: Representing the Urban Landscape*, edited by Keenan Norris, Scarecrow Press, 2014, pp. 9–18.

"Reviews." *Getting to Happy*, by Terry McMillan. *Publisher's Weekly*, July 2010, pp. 24–25.

Rice, E. Lacy. "The Color Purple" [A Review]. *WatchTCM*. https://www.tcm.com/watchtcm/titles/71239. Accessed June 17, 2023.

Richardson, Elaine. "To Protect and Serve: African American Female Literacies."
    College Composition and Communication, vol. 53, no. 4, June 2002, pp. 675–704.

Rosen, Judith. "Street Lit: Readers Gotta Have It." *Publisher's Weekly*, vol. 251,
    no. 50, December 13, 2004, pp. 31–35.

Salt-N-Pepa. "Let's Talk about Sex." *Blacks' Magic*. Next Plateau Records, 1991. CD.

Sapphire. *PUSH*. 1996. Vintage, 1997.

"Sapphire's Story: How *PUSH* Became *Precious*" [An Interview]. *NPR*, November 6,
    2009, www.npr.org/templates/story/story.php?storyId=120176695.

Schalk, Sami. *BodyMinds Reimagined: (Dis)ability, Race, and Gender in Black
    Women's Speculative Fiction*. Duke University Press, 2018.

Smith, Barbara. "Toward a Black Feminist Criticism." *African American Literary
    Theory: A Reader*, edited by Winston Napier, New York University Press, 2000,
    pp. 132–46.

Smith, Lillian. *Killers of the Dream*. W. W. Norton, 1949.

Souljah, Sister. *The Coldest Winter Ever*. 1999. Pocket Star Books, 2006.

Souljah, Sister. *Life After Death*. Emily Bestler Books, 2021.

Spillers, Hortense. "Interstices: A Small Drama of Words." *Pleasure and Danger:
    Exploring Female Sexuality*, edited by Carole Vance, Routledge, 1984, pp. 73–100.

Stepto, Robert. *From Behind the Veil*. University of Illinois Press, 1979.

"Steven Spielberg: Show Biz Interview (*The Color Purple*) 1985." *YouTube*,
    uploaded by DVDguy2021. www.youtube.com/watch?v=cbhFofvttAs. Accessed
    June 17, 2023.

Stockett, Kathryn. *The Help*. Berkley Books, 2009.

Tompkins, Lucille. Review of *Their Eyes Were Watching God*, by Zora Neale
    Hurston. *New York Times Book Review*, September 26, 1937. *Zora Neale
    Hurston: Critical Perspectives Past and Present*. Edited by Henry Louis Gates Jr.
    and K. A. Appiah, Amistad Press, 1993, pp. 18–19.

Towers, Robert. "Good Men Are Hard to Find." *New York Review of Books*, August 12,
    1982, www.nybooks.com/articles/1982/08/12/good-men-are-hard-to-find/.

Townsend, Tiffany G., et. al. "I'm No Jezebel; I Am Young, Gifted, and Black:
    Identity, Sexuality, and Black Girls." *Psychology of Women Quarterly*, vol. 34,
    2010, pp. 273–85.

Troutman, Denise. "The Tongue or the Sword: Which Is Master?" *African
    American Women Speak Out on Anita Hill-Clarence Thomas*, edited by
    Geneva Smitherman, Wayne State University Press, 1995, pp. 208–23.

Turner, Patricia A. *Ceramic Uncles and Celluloid Mammies*. Anchor Books, 1994.

Twitty, Michael W. "The Colonial Roots of Southern Barbeque: Re-Creating the
    Birth of an American Culinary Staple." *Afroculinaria*, July 14, 2012, afroculi
    naria.com/2012/07/14/the colonial-roots-of-southern-barbecue-re-creating
    -the-birth-of-an-american-culinary-staple/.

Valloro, Daniel R. "Lincoln, Stowe, and the 'Little Woman/Great War' Story: The Making, and Breaking, of a Great American Anecdote." *Journal of the Abraham Lincoln Association*, vol. 30, no. 1, 2009, pp. 18–34.

Vaughan, Alden T., and Virginia Mason Vaughan. "Before Othello: Elizabethan Representations of Sub-Saharan Africans." *William and Mary Quarterly*, Third Series, vol. 54, no. 1, 1997, pp. 19–44.

Veit-Wild, Flora, and Dirk Naguschewski. "Lifting the Veil of Secrecy." *Matatu: Journal for African Culture and Society*, no. 29/30, 2005, pp. ix–xxii.

Walker, Alice. *The Color Purple*. 1982. Harcourt, 2003.

Walker, Alice. *In Search of Our Mother's Gardens*. Harcourt, 1983.

Walker, Rebecca. "Lusting for Freedom." *Listen Up: Voices from the Next Feminist Generation*, edited by Barbara Findlen, Seal Press 2001, pp. 19–24.

Ward, Jesmyn. *Men We Reaped*. 2013. Bloomsbury, 2014.

Washington, Mary Helen. "The Darkened Eye Restored." 1987. *Reading Black, Reading Feminist: A Critical Anthology*, edited by Henry Louis Gates Jr., Meridian Books, 1990, pp. 30–43.

Washington, Mary Helen. "I Love the Way Janie Crawford Left Her Husbands: Zora Neale Hurston's Emergent Hero." 1987. *Zora Neale Hurston's Their Eyes Were Watching God: A Casebook*, edited by Cheryl Wall, Oxford University Press, 2000, pp. 27–40.

Watkins, Mel. "Some Letters Went to God." *New York Times Book Review*, July 25, 1982, p. 7.

Weir-Soley, Donna Aza. *Eroticisim, Spiritualilty and Resistance in Black Women's Writings*. University Press of Florida, 2009.

Wellington, Darryl Lorenzo. "Looking for Precious." *Crisis*, vol. 117, no. 1, 2010, p. 26.

White, Deborah Gray. *Ar'n't I a Woman?: Female Slaves in the Plantation South*. W. W. Norton, 1999.

Williams, Donna M. "Our Love/Hate Relationship with Zora Neale Hurston." *Black Collegian*, vol. 24, no. 3, 1994, p. 86.

Wilson, Lawrence. "Soul Attachment and Release." Center for Development, May 2011 and December 2017, https://drlwilson.com/articles/POSSESSION.htm.

Wright, Richard. "Between Laughter and Tears [Review]." *New Masses*, October 5, 1937. *Zora Neale Hurston: Critical Perspectives Past and Present*, edited by Henry Louis Gates Jr. and K. A. Appiah, Amistad Press, 1993, pp. 16–17.

Wright, Zachary. "It's Non-Negotiable. We Have to Teach Social Justice in Our Schools." *Education Post*, December 4, 2017, educationpost.org/its-non-negotiable-we-have-to-teach-social-justice-in-our-schools/.

INDEX

ABOUT THE AUTHOR

Dr. **Kemeshia Randle Swanson** is an associate professor of English at Gardner-Webb University in Boiling Springs, North Carolina. She earned her PhD in English at the University of Alabama. Dr. Swanson teaches and studies the intersections of Black feminisms, sexualities studies, critical race theory, popular culture, and the literary imagination. She has published peer-reviewed articles and book chapters, including "Gang Wars: The Academy vs. the Street" (2014), "The Sexless Servant Is the Safer Servant: Domesticated Domestics in Stockett's *The Help*" (2016), and "Lessons Learned, Degrees Earned: Street Literature, Black Bodies, and the Contemporary Academic Classroom" (2018).

www.ingramcontent.com/pod-product-compliance
Lightning Source LLC
Chambersburg PA
CBHW030334270326
41926CB00010B/1622